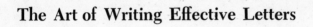

The Art of Writing Effective Letters

The Art of Writing
EFFECTIVE
LETTERS

ROSEMARY T. FRUEHLING

AND

SHARON BOUCHARD

McGRAW-HILL BOOK COMPANY

New York   St. Louis   San Francisco   Dusseldorf
London   Mexico   Sydney   Toronto

Contents

v

A Sneak Preview

Utilizing a slightly different approach in this preface, we are giving you a sneak preview of *The Art of Writing Effective Letters*—one that we hope will encourage you to actually become involved in the art of letter writing. In this book we have attempted to tell you an old story in a slightly new way—in an everyday, conversational, easy-to-read style.

Because we feel that people today are much more sophisticated—much more aware of the importance of good communications, both verbal and nonverbal—than they used to be, we decided that our approach should reflect this awareness. We knew that the best way of being "tuned out" by you, our reader, was to use the sermonlike approach that can be so deadly in "how to" books. Therefore, our first chapter, "Plan Ahead," allows you to dig right in and write a letter. Then, in the same chapter, you are provided a model to check the effectiveness of your writing.

Rather than to delve into such pompous and dull-sounding topics as "The Purpose of the Paragraph," "Unification of Thought," "Deletion of Irrelevant Material," "Logical Presentation of Ideas," "Importance of Conciseness," "Value of Tone," and "Reflection of Courtesy," we chose a more unconventional approach and substituted "So What's a Paragraph?" "United We Stand," "Stick to the Point," "Security Is . . . Being Tough," "Short and Sweet, Yet Vivid and Complete," and "It's All in How You Say It."

We have tried to say the things we had to say in a way that was easy to relate to. So, we presented the principles of good letter writing in Chapters 1 through 8. We seasoned these chapters with practical application, with good and sometimes bad examples, and with a checkpoint approach for easy evaluation.

In Chapter 9 basic principles of good letter writing are put into practice in the writing of routine request and reply letters. These principles are then applied in the writing of special-request and reply letters in Chapters 10 and 11. Although touched upon briefly prior to these chapters, the "you" attitude now becomes a way of thinking and a way of writing rather than the almost mechanical quality that is mentioned and soon forgotten in many business communications textbooks. It is no wonder so many have complained, "Of what value is it to change *me* to *you* or *I* to *you?*" when the importance of a writer's *attitude* toward his reader has not been sufficiently stressed or explained.

Chapter 12 gives you practice in writing goodwill, or "Just Plain Being Nice," letters. Sales letters are treated in their "Sock It to 'Em" context in Chapter 13 and are followed in Chapter 14 by how to complain when somebody has "goofed."

Letters that say "I'm short on cash but long on character—therefore, I hope to get credit" will inevitably lead to some collection attempts through letters that say "Pay Up." Why? Just because not everybody is perfect—right? Obviously, the applications in which we have attempted to involve you in Chapters 15 and 16 should be of considerable value.

Chapter 17 is an attempt to gain total commitment through involvement of oneself—a job application package called "Here Comes the Judge" because it actually will be the judge of your letter-writing ability. Someday, someplace, you will want some job very badly. This will require putting your best foot forward in an application letter.

Briefly in Chapter 18 we have attempted to introduce informal report writing with a "Size It Up" approach.

Needless to say, many people contributed to this book. We are most grateful to our husbands, our children, our colleagues, and to our friends in business who were most helpful and who became involved with us in this project.

ROSEMARY T. FRUEHLING
SHARON BOUCHARD

1

Plan Ahead

How Would You Tackle It?

Having just returned from a hectic shopping trip with at least six stops for errands and whatnots, Mrs. Anthony decides to make a last stop at the mailbox to pick up the mail. Among all the "junk mail," periodicals, monthly bills, and so on, she notices a very businesslike-looking envelope addressed to her. She hurriedly tears it open and reads its contents:

Mrs. Elizabeth Anthony
President of the League of Women Voters
6 Jersey Avenue
Hopkins, MN 55343

Dear Mrs. Anthony:

Will you please accept this invitation to be the guest speaker at the Minnesota Office Education Association Leadership Conference Awards Banquet to be held on April 10, 19—, at 8:30 P.M., in the Minnesota Suite of the Mall Hotel in St. Paul?

This banquet is the culminating function of a three-day conference where 2,000 office-occupations high school students from the state have been competing in contests to measure achievement in office skills. Awards will be presented to the first-, second-, and third-place winners by the State Supervisor of Business and Office Occupations.

Your address should reflect the importance of competition to our society and should be approximately 30 minutes in length.

Please indicate what the honorarium and travel expenses would be. If possible, please confirm by March 10.

Sincerely yours,
David Anderson
State President

The invitation is Mrs. Anthony's first piece of official business since being elected to her new position, president of the League of Women Voters. Of course, she will accept the invitation and is anxious about her talk—and a bit excited—but the problem at hand is how best to answer her first business letter. Certainly, she has written business letters before; but, somehow, this is different. She doesn't want to scribble a "yes" and the title of her presentation, "Competition is the Essence of the American Economy," on the letter and mail it back to David Anderson. What would this young man think of her; and more important, what would he think of the organization she has been chosen to head? She rereads the letter and thinks, "David Anderson sounds like a very bright young adult. His letter is clear, easy to read, and he gets right to the point in a courteous manner. As soon as I get into the house, I must answer him in the same way. It shouldn't be too tough, should it?"

Assume the role of Mrs. Anthony. How would you tackle it?

Would You Dig Right In?

Let's assume that you, like Mrs. Anthony, have decided to just sit down and write, without first planning your reply. She wanted to "dig right in" and cut all the "red tape" usually involved in business letter writing. Try answering the letter to that bright-sounding young man, David Anderson, in this fashion. Seriously, jot down an answer to him on a sheet of paper, right now.

Plan Ahead—Why?

When you have completed your letter, answer the following questions, and you will begin to see why planning before writing is a must in business communication.

1. How much time did writing the message to David Anderson require? Could you afford to spend that much time on each message you write? Do you suppose that Mrs. Anthony will be able to spend as much time on each piece of correspondence that she will receive in her new position?

2. Does your message provide all the information David Anderson will need? In your letter, did you include all these topics? Check those you omitted.

_a. Appreciation for showing interest in you and your organization

_b. Clear acceptance of the invitation

_c. Title of the presentation and general information regarding its coverage

_d. Honorarium

_e. The time of arrival (speakers are usually seated at the head table)

_f. Biographical sketch for publicity purposes

3. Are the topics you discussed arranged in a forward-moving, smooth-flowing sequence? Although there is no one way to organize topics related to a particular subject, whatever method is used should make it easy for David Anderson to quickly and accurately follow your thinking.

4. Is your message geared to the needs and interests of David Anderson—or could it have been written to almost anyone? An effective business communication reflects the writer's total appreciation of the reader as a unique person.

5. Does your message indicate that you had a specific purpose in writing? Did you in essence say "I am delighted to accept your invitation..."? Although some communications have no purpose other than gaining the reader's goodwill, most attempt to sell a product or service, to settle a claim, or to accomplish a similar objective as well as to build goodwill. A message that has no clearly identifiable purpose or objective represents a waste of time for both the writer and the reader.

6. Does your message make it clear what response, if any, the reader should make? For example, is the honorarium acceptable? Also, if a letter describes a sale or a meeting that is to be held on Thursday and Friday of next week, it should also indicate what you want the reader to do in connection with the sale or meeting. Again, any communication that leads the reader to ask himself "So what?" is a waste of his and the writer's time.

Plan—When? How?

The need for planning *before* writing is no doubt becoming clear to you—but it is of such vital importance to effective business writing that it merits restating as a cardinal rule: *Always plan before writing*. While planning does not absolutely guarantee, it does provide reasonable assurance, that every letter, memo, report, or other communication you write is not only worthwhile but also as effective as you can make it.

When you are answering a letter, for example, you have a concrete source of information that you can consult as you:

1. State your purpose in writing.

2. Determine what response, if any, you would like your reader to make.

3. Decide the main subject of your letter and the topics related to it that you will need to present and discuss in order to write a complete message. (When replying to correspondence, many successful writers simply underline or jot in the margin the topics they will need to cover.)

4. Decide the best sequence for presenting and discussing the topics you have underlined or listed; then number or letter them in an informal outline form. Check to see that each topic is relevant—omit those that are not.

5. Consider your reader and, in every way possible, plan your message from his point of view.

If you are initiating correspondence, all you need to do is modify the steps you would take if you were answering a letter or a memo. Particularly at the outset, you will find it helpful to develop a written working outline that includes:

(1) a complete statement of your purpose in writing

(2) the response you want your reader to make

(3) the subject of your message and the topics you will need to present and discuss

(4) a quick sketch—based on whatever information you can gain from sources that are accessible to you—of your reader.

If you don't personally know your reader, or if you have no ready sources of information about him—and you often will be writing under such circumstances—there's nothing you can do but use your best judgment in planning a reader-oriented communication.

By planning, and following the steps discussed, Mrs. Anthony's response to David Anderson could have sounded like this:

Dear David:

Thank you for inviting me to speak to the office-occupations high school students attending the Minnesota Office Education Association Leadership Conference at the Mall Hotel in St. Paul, Minnesota, on April 10, 19 __ at 8:30 P.M. As president of the League of Women

Voters, an organization devoted to the principles of the competitive system, and as a courtesy of the League, I am delighted to accept your invitation at no expense to you.

The title of my 30-minute discussion is "Competition Is the Essence of the American Economy." Since the group is large, I will highlight my talk with twelve color slides. Will it be possible for you to arrange for a screen and projection table located in the best viewing position? I will provide my own remote-control projector and slides, of course.

Should I arrive prior to 8:30 P.M. to facilitate seating arrangements? Will it be possible for you to send me a program beforehand so that I may brief myself on the order of events?

Enclosed is my photograph and biographical sketch, which can be used both for publicity and for any introductory remarks you may wish to make.

Best wishes, David, for a successful conference. I am looking forward to being a small part of it.

Cordially yours,
Elizabeth Anthony

2

So What's a Paragraph?

Now that you have established the purpose of your letter, outlined the content and organization of your message, and considered your reader and the response you wish him to make, you are ready to present your thoughts in effective language form.

Since elementary school you have been learning to write grammatically correct, forceful sentences. With this skill you have the basis for good writing. You need more, however, for good writing requires more than good sentences. You must develop the skill of combining sentences into logical paragraphs of well-organized messages. In this section you will learn the purpose of paragraphing, the importance of topic sentences to both writer and reader, and the value of correctly expressing the ideas you wish to convey.

Why Paragraph?

There are several reasons for paragraphing. The paragraph is one way to improve the general attractiveness of your business letter, to make it look inviting to your reader. It should look

7

easy to read even before actual reading. Such things as wide-enough margins, short and medium-length paragraphs, and tabulated material all make a letter inviting. On the other hand, long, involved paragraphs look monotonous and forbidding.

The paragraph may also be used to highlight a statement or question. The technique of enumerating points by paragraphing (treating each point as a separate paragraph) makes it easy for the reader to recognize and answer them.

Probably the most important reason for paragraphing is to signal to your reader that you wish to begin a new idea. Actually, it is a matter of both thought and structural unity—the grouping of sentences to develop a clearly defined thought. By paragraphing, you make it easy for the reader to follow your thinking and for you to lead him through your organized message.

Developing a complete thought through the grouping of sentences brings us to an important subject—the topic sentence.

Big Deal—A Topic Sentence

A topic sentence is the "big deal" in a paragraph. It often appears at the beginning of the paragraph and capstones the unit of thought. It helps your reader to grasp easily and quickly the main thought of the paragraph, and it helps you restrict your statements to those that are related and relevant to the main thought. The topic sentence is the nucleus of an effective paragraph, and all other paragraph sentences should relate to the topic sentence. Your reader will decide on the basis of this sentence what he thinks the major topic is, and he will expect you to stick to that topic.

Read the following letter and notice how difficult it is to read and to find the topic sentences because of poor paragraphing.

Dear Mr. Jones:

Since your policy contains an Automatic Premium Loan Clause, we can arrange to have your premiums paid by loan provided there is enough cash value in your policy. Then you can simply make repayments toward your loan and all will be in order. I'm sorry that we cannot arrange to have you pay premiums on the monthly basis, as you asked, but monthly premiums must amount to at least $10. However, this Automatic Premium Loan arrangement will, in effect, accomplish the same thing. Let us know if you want us to do this, won't you? It will be a pleasure to take care of it for you.

Sincerely yours,

Now read the revised letter. Through paragraphing and good use of topic sentences, the letter is more attractive and much easier to read and understand. It makes it easier for the reader to respond.

Dear Mr. Jones:

You will be pleased to know that because you have an Automatic Premium Loan Clause policy and a cash value of $1,200, we can make your annual premium by loan.

If your premium was $10 or over, we could arrange to pay your premiums monthly. Since your premium is only $6 a month, you may have a loan for the total premium of $72, and you may repay it when possible.

All you need to do is check and sign the enclosed card and mail it back today, and your premium is paid in full.

The Long and Short of It

The length of your paragraphs will be governed by the subject you are writing about and the number and nature of the comments you need to make about it. If it is absolutely necessary to have long paragraphs in a letter, deliberately season the letter with short paragraphs of two or three lines to bring your reader's interest back. A good rule to remember is that a short paragraph invites reading and makes a stronger impression. Therefore, it is wise to make opening and closing paragraphs short—probably from one to five lines.

Now What?

So you realize that you do need paragraphs and that the topic sentence is a "big deal" in each paragraph. Now what? Now you must consider the various ways to develop effective paragraphs.

Tell Me a Story

If you are writing about something that has already happened or if you wish to develop an idea vividly, you may wish to use the "storytelling" approach. For example:

At 4:30 P.M. on Wednesday, March 13, I was traveling east on Excelsior Boulevard and slowly approached the stop sign at Alabama Avenue. I was suddenly struck from the rear, causing me to hit the car in front of me.

You may also wish to use the storytelling approach to develop an idea step by step. For example:

To preplan an effective business letter, you must first decide on the purpose of your letter and then visualize your reader as an individual by considering the situation from the reader's point of view. Next, you must consider the best appeal for your specific reader—psychological or logical appeal. After you decide upon the best appeal, you must fit the tone and vocabulary of your letter to your reader.

Draw Me a Picture

If you are writing about a product, you may present your message most effectively in "descriptive" paragraphs. For example:

The Maneuverable Can Opener is a quality product with magic magnetic fingers to hold the lid after it is cut around. Famous "Voodoo-Gears" keep the cutting wheel sharp, open cans of all sizes, and swing away when not in use.

Break It Up

If you wish to categorize or list the data about a subject, you may wish to use the "break it up" approach. For example:

At present nearly 100 per cent of safety razor sales are divided among three major brands: (1) Clean-Shave razors are all designed to take standard single-edged blades. (2) Sharpee razors are designed to take the double-edged blade. (3) Close-up razors are an injector-type razor which permit special thin, single-edged blades to be injected directly into the razors.

What's the Advantage?

If you wish to convince your reader of the advantages of your product or idea, you may wish to use the "what's the advantage?" approach. For example:

You will find that the Michel Ten-Key Adding Machine has many advantages over the full-bank adding machine that you are now using. First of all, you must realize that more speed may be attained by operating by touch. The Michel Ten-Key allows the operator to look at the copy. Much time is lost as the eyes move from copy to keyboard.

Prove It

If you are writing in an attempt to persuade your reader through inductive reasoning to arrive at a general conclusion based on specific facts, you may wish to use the "prove it" approach. For example:

The number of typewriters imported into the United States is rapidly increasing. Many different typewriters manufactured in European countries—Italy, Germany, England—are seen in American businesses. This means that the American public is favoring more and more foreign-made products.

You may also wish to use the "prove it" approach to persuade your reader through deductive reasoning to apply a general principle to a particular situation. For example:

It seems obvious that every school should require every student to complete classes that will be useful to him in everyday living. Just about everyone writes business letters in his everyday living. The knowledge and practice needed to develop letter-writing skills are extremely valuable. Therefore, our schools should adopt measures which will require all students to complete a course in "Business Correspondence Writing."

Using one of the methods of paragraph development described in this chapter—"Prove It"—notice how the topic sentence below, "Business letter writing is the key to success," can be developed through *inductive reasoning*.

"Business letter writing is the key to success." Since we live in a business world where thousands of letters are written daily, effective letter writing will be necessary if we are to achieve everyday living success.

Can you identify the method of paragraph development used in the following illustrative paragraphs? Check up on yourself and then verify your answers.

a. Early this morning the white mists were lifting their curtains to reveal the blue-green Catskills in the distance. In this setting your summer home is at its loveliest.

b. I have been receiving copies of *Effective Writing* for years. And somewhere along the line the magazine started coming addressed to Miss Julie Cary. My mother told me I was always intended to be a girl, but I assure you there is nothing feminine about me.

c. First, you must oil the machine thoroughly; second, you must check all electrical connections; third, you should make sure that all safety jackets are securely attached.

Paragraph A utilized a descriptive approach; paragraph B used a storytelling approach; and paragraph C used a categorizing approach.

For further practice and to make you more aware of your own paragraph development, select sales letters, circulars, or any other correspondence and try to identify the methods of paragraph development discussed in this chapter. In most cases, you will be delighted with your success in recognizing one of the five methods discussed. In others, it may be difficult, simply because many poorly developed paragraphs never accomplish their objectives—meaning and understanding.

3

United We Stand . . .

"United we stand, divided we fall!" This famous adage directly applies to effective paragraph development in business communications. Unification must apply to individual sentences, to individual paragraphs, and to the total message. Whereas in a theme or essay you have one main idea with all paragraphs relating to that one idea, in business letter writing you may have a number of varied ideas in one piece of correspondence. In the letter of application, for example, the purpose of the first paragraph is to make known the fact that you are applying for a specific position. The purpose of the last paragraph is to request a personal interview. The purpose of an in-between paragraph may be to provide personal recommendations. Each of these paragraphs deals with a different topic, but the unity of this letter lies in the fact that the various topics or ideas all relate to the applicant.

Let's Be Logical

It is also important that you omit irrelevant ideas from your paragraphs. You can avoid this pitfall by careful planning so as to present ideas logically. To achieve unity, you must establish a logical sequence for your paragraphs. Once again referring to the letter of application, it would be important for you to decide which of your qualifications are most relevant to the particular position. In considering your qualifications, it would not be worthwhile to write a lengthy paragraph elaborating on your stamp collection if, for example, you were applying for a job as a salesman. You must also present your qualifications in logical order: educational experience, work experience, references, and so on.

Presenting your ideas in logical sequence will ensure unity of your thoughts and ideas. It will also assure your reader that he is going somewhere. He will be able to follow your path and separate your major points from the details. To make sure he can do so, you will have to consider the situation from the reader's point of view and be sure to:

1. Begin by telling him the purpose of your communication.
2. Plan your letter and present your ideas in logical sequence to serve this purpose.

Do not allow your reader to follow wrong paths in your writing. Organize or unite your writing so that he will be led along the right path. Include what you feel is the best appeal to suit your reader, and you will give your communications an air of readability, which is one mark of effective letter writing.

To develop this point of presenting paragraphs logically, let's assume that you and your wife are the owners of the Dawson's Furniture Store. You have received a check for $24 from Mr. John Leonard in payment of his monthly installment on the French Provincial bedroom set that he and his wife purchased last August. This is his fourth payment; he has two payments left. When you go to record his check, you find that this month's payment (December's) was paid by his wife on December 2. The next payment is not due until January 6. You are to write

Mr. Leonard a letter of explanation and enclose his check for $24.

First, you should jot down the main ideas of the letter you will write. Omit any of the irrelevant information given you in the explanation above. Do not read ahead of this paragraph until you have made a list of your ideas.

Did you include any of the following ideas? They are not relevant. If you included them, cross them off your list.

a. This is your fourth of six payments.
b. Bedroom set was purchased last August.
c. You checked the records and found that the payment was on a French Provincial bedroom set.

You should have included these ideas:

d. Thank you for check.
e. December payment for bedroom set.
f. Enclosing check.
g. Wife made payment.
h. Next payment January 6.

Carefully look at the ideas you want to include in your letter to Mr. Leonard. Think of the relationship of one idea to another. Organize your ideas in a logical sequence. Now write a letter to Mr. Leonard on a sheet of paper.

Did you:

(1) Combine the "thank you" and "December payment for bedroom set" in your first sentence?

(2) Realize that idea g (wife's payment) is the reason for idea f (enclosing check)?

(3) Combine ideas f and g in one sentence to show that relationship?

Following is a good example of how this letter might be written. How does yours compare?

Dear Mr. Leonard:

Thank you for your check for the December payment on your bedroom set. However, I am enclosing your check because your wife paid this installment on December 2.

Your next payment is due on January 6.

Sincerely yours,

Notice how the following message is not united, coherent, or in a logical sequence.

We received your letter dated January 10 in which you ask for our advice concerning the buying and selling of securities. We are pleased to be able to be of help to you in any way possible, since that is the reason we are in business in today's busy world. We will be very happy to answer any questions you might think of sometime later.

Answers to your questions in your January 10 letter may be found in our booklet for beginners in the stock market business of buying and selling securities. Our local consultant for your particular territory could also be of great help, we are sure.

Now look at the same letter rewritten. See how it has been improved through unity, coherence, and the logical sequence of ideas.

Thank you for your letter of January 10 asking our advice on the buying and selling of securities.

Enclosed is a free copy of our booklet *You Should Be Interested in Buying and Selling Securities.* This informative booklet does a thorough job of acquainting prospective investors with the stock market.

If you wish to have one of our local consultants help you regarding the great adventure of investing, return the enclosed, stamped card and he will set up an appointment with you.

Now let's consider a situation which may well arise, since many of us belong to civic, social, and church organizations.

The following example illustrates a request for information regarding fund-raising projects.

This message is difficult to read and understand because it is not unified in thought or logical in sequence.

I have been asked to write to your company on behalf of our organization to ask you how we can improve the condition of our local fund-raising projects, which are not doing the job for our group that we think they should be. We feel your experience could help us get back on the right track. We would like to receive any of your suggestions that would be helpful to us in attempting to improve the condition of our problem.

Please send us your booklets or pamphlets on fund-raising projects for small clubs, and I will present your ideas at our next meeting on Thursday at 8 P.M. so that our committee can begin to reorganize our strategy of attack. We know there must be a solution because we have heard about the successes other clubs have had after they have written to your company, the "ABC" Organizer, for advice. Thus, we, too, are writing to you for advice.

The next example is a letter requesting the same information; however, this letter is clear, coherent, and logical. Doesn't it make a whale of a difference?

You have helped many clubs improve their fund-raising projects. Won't you please help the Parsippany High School Chapter of the Distributive Education Clubs of America?

Any information you can provide me will help, as I have been asked by our president to present ideas in a committee report next Tuesday, April 8, at 8 P.M.

Also, if you have any booklets or pamphlets on fund-raising projects, I will be happy to purchase them and arrange to pick them up.

4

Stick to the Point

Aren't you annoyed to the point of "tuning out" a speaker who does not "stick to the point" of his verbal message? Your reader, also, will be annoyed to the point of throwing out your written message if you do not stick to the point.

Say Just Enough

When writing business communications, stick to the point and omit unnecessary repetitions and irrelevant or superfluous words and phrases that contribute to making messages long and pompous. Whereas in theme writing such devices are sometimes helpful in creating a specific style, in business correspondence they are never desirable. Remember to say just enough to achieve the purpose of your message. When you have done this, you have attained unity and organization and avoided the jargon which is often considered the "grand style," or the antiquated business style of writing.

Following is the "Jargoneer's Checklist" taken from the *Jargoneer's Handbook*, a guide for apprentices who wish to

achieve this so-called grand style. How do you rate as a jargoneer?

JARGONEER'S CHECKLIST

1. Since original thoughts are hard to think of, use a cliché whenever possible.

2. Always substitute an archaic, pompous word for a contemporary,
conversational word.

3. Use the general word instead of the specific. This keeps the
reader awake, guessing at your meaning.

4. If you can think of a long, complicated word to take the place of
a short, simple word, use the inflated word.

5. Make all active sentences passive.

6. Choose one type of sentence construction and never vary from
it. This gives your letters a dull, monotonous tone which has a certain
dignity.

Now that you know the basic tenets of the jargoneer, take a
look at some of the following outmoded words and phrases, unnecessary repetitions, and overworked words and phrases that
he never misses a chance to use.

OUTMODED WORDS AND PHRASES

Outmoded	*Suggested Substitutions*
Are in a position to	Can
At an early date	Soon (or give exact date)
At that time	Then
At this time, at the present time, at the present writing	Now, at present
Due to the fact that	As, because, since
Enclosed please find	Enclosed is
In accordance with your request	As you requested
In order to	To
In regard to	About
In the event that	In case, if
Meets with your approval	You like, is satisfactory
Recent date	(Give exact date—June 10)
The writer	I, me
Under separate cover	By freight (or whatever means of sending)

Up to this writing	Previously
Wish to acknowledge	Your letter of July 10
Your check in the amount of	Your check for

UNNECESSARY REPETITIONS

Avoid	*Use*	*Avoid*	*Use*
And etc.	Etc.	Final completion	Completion
At about	About	Lose out	Lose
Both alike	Alike	May perhaps	May
Check into	Check	Near to	Near
Complete monopoly	Monopoly	New beginner	Beginner
Continue on	Continue	Over with	Over
Cooperate together	Cooperate	Past experience	Experience
Customary practice	Practice	Rarely ever	Rarely
Depreciate in value	Depreciate	Refer back	Refer
During the course of	During	Same identical	Identical
Endorse on the back	Endorse	Up above	Above

OVERWORKED WORDS AND PHRASES

Overworked	*Suggested Substitutions*
Along the lines of	Like
At all times	Always
By means of	By
In the near future	(State the approximate or exact time)
Inasmuch as	Since
Awful	Terrifying
Bad	Inexcusable
Fabulous	Spectacular
Good	Choice
Lively	Delightful

Notice how the following sentences can be rewritten to delete irrelevant material. Also note how appropriate words are substituted for unnecessary repetitions.

1a. We acknowledge your order and assure you same will have our immediate attention.

1b. Your order for two beach towels, No. 646 @ $2.95, will be delivered to you today and billed to your account.

2a. I would like to take the liberty of asking that you grant me an interview.

2b. May I come in for an interview?

3a. We are pleased to advise that our prices are as low as those of any other candy jobber.

3b. Look at the enclosed price list and you can see our prices are as low as those of any other jobber in the city.

4a. We acknowledge receipt of your letter of July 21, with reference to the balance of your account in the amount of $750.

4b. Thank you for your letter of July 21 referring to your balance of $750.

5a. We had started to commence the necessary processing required to establish the amount of your refund.

5b. Your refund of $80 has been credited to your account and will appear on your July statement.

6a. We wish to advise you that the subject amount will appear as a credit to you on your next rendered bill.

6b. You will have a credit balance of $8.60 appear on your July statement.

7a. Arrangements have been duly made to reestablish your service according to our practice regarding same.

7b. You will be enjoying soft water again on Saturday, July 9.

8a. With reference to your past communication to us, our records show that your deposit was returned because you canceled the order.

8b. Your deposit of $40 was returned to you on the same day you canceled your order, July 7.

9a. Will you please send me a sample for butchers of your casing that will be suitable for stuffing sausage in.

9b. Will you please send me a sample of your 2-inch sausage casing.

    10a. What will be the entitlement of your speech?
    10b. What is the name of your speech?

Follow the Leader

    Just as all groups, both informal and formal, need a leader, so do your paragraphs. A good selection of linking words and other transitional devices, which are the informal and formal leaders of your paragraphs, will allow your reader to follow your ideas from paragraph to paragraph and give your letter the quality of coherence.

    Transitional words, phrases, and sentences are considered mechanical aids in linking your major and minor topics. Examples of transitional words are *and, also, but, however, thus, therefore, first, second,* and *finally.* Examples of transitional phrases are *so that, in order to, for example, on the contrary, in particular, as well as, in addition,* and *due to.*

    Don't make the mistake of expecting these transitional aids to perform miracles. As already stated, unless your ideas follow a logical sequence, no transitional device used will fool your reader. Just as the public speaker who rambles on from one thought to another without coherence fails to integrate his message for his listener, so will you as a writer fail to integrate your message for your reader.

    Emphasizing key words and phrases by repetition is another way to achieve coherence, as illustrated in the following paragraph:

    Examples of transitional words and phrases are "first," "for example," "therefore," and "finally." These transitional words and phrases help the reader make a smooth transition from one paragraph to another. Such devices should be used in business writing.

    The use of pronouns is another way of gaining coherence in your business correspondence. Pronouns can be repeated with-it, and they and such pronoun forms as him, his, her, its, and them is less tedious than the repetition of nouns.

Coherently using transitional devices, logically presenting ideas, and saying just enough to achieve the purpose of your message are techniques that will strengthen the organization of your message.

Lincoln's "Gettysburg Address" is a masterpiece of coherence because of his excellent use of transitional devices. Notice also the logical order in which he presented his ideas. (Each sentence is presented as a separate paragraph to facilitate reading, and the transitional words have been underscored.)

GETTYSBURG ADDRESS

Fourscore and seven years ago our fathers brought forth on this continent a new nation, conceived in liberty, and dedicated to the proposition that all men are created equal.

Now we are engaged in a great civil war, testing whether that nation, or any nation so conceived and so dedicated, can long endure.

We are met on a great battlefield of that war.

We have come to dedicate a portion of that field, as a final resting place for those who here gave their lives that that nation might live.

It is altogether fitting and proper that we should do this.

But, in a larger sense, we cannot dedicate—we cannot consecrate—we cannot hallow. . . .

5

Security Is . . . Being Tough

"Security is . . . being tough" or being in command of the situation. Up to this point we have considered unity, the logical presentation of ideas, coherence, and saying just enough to achieve the purpose of your message. Although these elements are vital, they alone will not ensure an effective business communication. You must also take command and present your ideas with force.

Where the Action Is

One of the best ways to achieve forcefulness is to avoid excessive use of nonaction verbs, which usually result in too much wordiness. Messages that lack color or that are tedious and vague are often the result of nonaction. Business letter writing lends itself to the excessive use of nonaction verbs, because a writer often does not want to commit himself; therefore, he is unwilling to be specific. For example, "It is noted that your sales have not quite met the January quota" could be stated actively: "Your sales *are $200* short of the January quota." If you are *forced* to be tactful and noncommittal, you must use nonaction verbs. It is important, however, to make the use of nonaction verbs the exception rather than the rule.

Another way to add vitality and force to your writing is to use *action verbs* in place of *nouns*. For example, "The state requirement is 2,000 clock hours of work experience" could be vividly stated: "The state requires 2,000 clock hours of on-the-job training in an office occupation." Simply replacing the noun *requirement* with the verb *requires* allows the subject *state* to take command of the action of the sentence.

Security Is . . . Strategic Planning

"Security is . . . strategic planning" and presenting your paragraphs to ensure forcefulness. It will be up to you to phrase and to place important points in strategic positions to get and retain your reader's interest. For example, the statement "Will you please consider me an applicant for the position of clerk-typist in your payroll department as advertised in the December 15 *New York Times*" is placed early in the letter so as to give the reader a clear indication of the purpose of the letter. Contrast this to the following wishy-washy manner of application: "After reading your advertisement for a clerk-typist in the daily newspaper, I decided that the position is most appealing."

The first example considers the situation from the reader's point of view. The writer assumes that the reader is a busy person, eager to learn the purpose of correspondence he is reading. Formal application is made forcefully and early in the letter. But the second example does not consider the situation from the reader's point of view. It is wordy and vague; it does not forcefully state the purpose of the correspondence. The impact of your letter will be determined by the power, or forcefulness, of your paragraphs.

Well-organized business letter writing depends on clear thinking and planning before writing. If you are answering a letter, you should read the letter carefully and reread it if necessary. Sometimes incoming correspondence is unclear, and several readings are necessary for complete understanding. This rereading may save you writing a follow-up letter.

A good practice is to underscore main ideas of the letter to be answered. This procedure will give you, at a quick glance, the essential ideas around which you can organize your answer. Then, of course, if you restrict your reply to these ideas, you will have a complete, concise, and forceful message. If you are initiating correspondence, you should jot down the points you wish to cover, get all the background material you can, look critically at the ideas you have, and choose only those that are relevant to the purpose of your message. Remember to sort important ideas and thoughts from irrelevant ones.

Consider the following paragraph. Notice how it rambles.

We acknowledge receipt of your letter of January 10, making application for credit. We want you to understand clearly that your account with us will carry a top limit of $200 and that our statements, sent on the last day of each month, are payable by the tenth of the following month. We hope you will enjoy the privileges of your credit with us. We are glad to grant you the credit that you recently asked for.

Obviously a more forceful, positive way of announcing such good news to a customer is as follows:

Congratulations! Your application for credit of $200 has been granted. Statements will be sent out the last day of each month and are payable within 10 days.

Well-chosen short words are usually stronger and more meaningful than longer ones. Since words of one syllable make up 80 to 90 percent of our language, include at least 60 percent one-syllable words in the sentence structure of your business correspondence. Of course, the more smoothly the sentence flows, the more easily the reader understands the message.

Pay special attention to making the first and last sentences of your letter the most forceful. The first sentence, as already stated, should reflect a "you" attitude. Just as important, it should indicate the purpose of the correspondence and refer briefly to any previous message by date so that the recipient may easily refer to a file copy. With the same forcefulness, the last sentence should courteously summarize the message and emphasize the action you desire.

Remember, an expression such as "Hoping to have an interview with you soon, I remain" is a weak ending that lacks force and violates effective letter-writing rules. Avoid monotony; use variety. Present new ideas with strength. Strategically plan each paragraph to convey your message precisely and retain your reader's interest.

6

Short and Sweet, Yet Vivid and Complete

Happiness Is . . . "You" and "Yours"

"Service is our job; courtesy is our goal." A leading national insurance company spends thousands of dollars promoting this motto and training its employees to follow its message. You are aware of the importance of courtesy ("being sweet") in everyday living. Are you aware, however, how equally important courtesy is in business correspondence? The recipient of many business communications has never seen the writer nor the organization he represents. Can you see then how important it is that every piece of correspondence which leaves the desk of the writer reflects courteousness?

Please and *thank you* are considered courteous phrases, but do they ensure a proper display of respect, concern, consideration, and helpfulness? The intangible qualities of courteousness can best be achieved if you will remember that all correspondence must be written from the reader's point of view. The reader's point of view is really the "you" attitude, or seeing things through the reader's eyes.

"I want to get a part-time selling job with your firm so that I may earn money to enroll at the University this fall" is certainly not considering the reader's point of view or using the "you" attitude.

"Will you please consider me for the part-time selling vacancy in your firm. I plan to attend the University this fall and need to earn money to pay for my college expenses" incorporates the word *please* and uses the word *you;* however, it still lacks the intangible qualities of courtesy, which considers the reader's point of view.

Let us try to change the paragraph not only by adding a courteous *please* and using the word *you*, but also by considering the reader. "Will you please consider my application for the part-time salesman position with your firm. Since I plan to major in marketing and merchandising at the University this fall, you can be sure that I would be an enthusiastic trainee, eager to learn selling."

Any employer would certainly be more impressed with the last illustration, because this writer has indicated how he would be an asset to the employer's firm.

If you are to consider the reader's point of view, you must always assume that as a successful businessman, he is extremely busy. He is not too busy, however, to recognize the benefits or profits that could be his if he hires a promising applicant or sends the materials requested or replaces a defective product manufactured by his company.

Would You Believe ... a Letter Can Smile?

To generate the "you" attitude, you must learn to forget yourself and put yourself in your reader's shoes. This is not an easy task; however, it can be accomplished. In your everyday encounters, the person with whom you communicate can see a smile, see a gesture of good manners, and hear the pleasant inflection of your voice. You must learn to write with your smile and good manners. If you have an artificial smile on your face, you will soon be detected; if you have an artificial smile in your letter, you will also be detected. Can you imagine how much more important the smile in your written communications must be? You may not get another opportunity to smile.

To interest yourself in others is the first step you must take to master the art of developing the "you" attitude. Are you not impressed with the person who remembers to call you by name shortly after an introduction or by a person who remembers your hobby is skiing? Why? Because that person has taken an interest in you as an individual.

"We would like to have you send 75 copies of your *Training Salesmen* pamphlet by September 17" states a request completely. However, "Your pamphlet *Training Salesmen* is recognized as one of the finest sales-training booklets available. Will you please send me 75 copies by September 17" shows you have taken an interest in your reader, and such a request will probably ensure an enthusiastic and prompt reply.

"Me" or "You"?

Since we have established that any reader is concerned with himself, we can begin to convey the "you" attitude simply by using the word *you* rather than *me* whenever possible.

Me	You
I want to thank you	Thank you
I wish to order	Will you please send
I am replying to your letter	Your letter
Our firm would like to order	Will you please send
I wish to be considered an applicant	Will you please consider me an applicant

It just stands to reason that *you, your,* and *yours* will be accepted more enthusiastically than such pronouns as *I, me, we,* and *our.* Remember the reader's point of view? You must make sure that what you have to say is of value to the reader and that your reader is the center of attention.

No Pseudo-You

You—you—you sprinkled in every sentence of your message, however, will not ensure the "you" attitude. To revise a sentence in an attempt to change words to *you* or *your* is only the first step. To change "I wish to have a reply by June 10" to "Your reply by June 10 is requested by me" is ridiculous and awkward and should be avoided. It is possible to adopt the "you" attitude in your letter without using the pronoun *you.* "A reply by June 10 would ensure the success of our sales meeting" illustrates the subtle use of the "you" attitude.

Many writers seem to feel that in a letter of application or in one requesting goods or services they can kill two birds with one stone with a "Thank you in advance." The phrase *thank you* is courteous; however, isn't it rather presumptuous, or taking things for granted, to say "Will you please send me 75 copies of your pamphlet" in the first paragraph of a letter and to say "thank you" in the last paragraph of the same letter? Have you given the recipient a chance to say "No"? The practice of thanking in advance is offensive to many readers. Never thank any correspondent until your request has been met. It is never necessary for you to thank a reader for his time, such as "I appreciate any consideration you give this matter." No matter how sure you are that your request will be met, give your reader the privilege of decision.

Just as the formal politeness of a new acquaintance does not generate a genuine friendship, the mechanical placement of *you, please,* and *thank you* in your writing does not guarantee a "you" attitude.

A *properly* developed "you" attitude will get a *do* response from your reader, whether it be sending you the requested literature or buying your product.

Consider the following bank letter. It is full of "we" attitude, useless words, and seeming irritation.

Dear Mr. Jacobs:

We have, in the past, written many times suggesting the transfer of certain securities from our name to yours, since you are the beneficiary under Mr. Smith's will. From time to time, dividend checks come to us because the securities remain untransferred. The stocks to which we refer are the Silver Oil Company and Purchase Oil and Refinery, Inc.

We will appreciate it very much if you will bring in the above securities so that transfers can be made and dividends paid on the stocks can be sent to you instead of to us.

We would like to get rid of this extra handling and shall gladly do so as soon as you bring the securities to us.

Sincerely yours,

Notice how the same message can be rewritten with a "you" attitude. Irrelevant words have been eliminated to make the message clearer and more meaningful. .

Would you like to receive your Silver Oil Company and Purchase Oil and Refinery, Inc., monthly dividend checks a week earlier than you have been receiving them?

If you will bring the securities and stop in at our office at 214 Broadway, we will quickly transfer them from our name to your name as requested in Mr. Smith's will.

It isn't necessary to make an appointment. Just drop in for a few minutes to make sure your dividend checks will be mailed directly to you next month.

Slice to Be Concise

Another way you can help your written message to accomplish its purpose is to be concise or to make it *short*. You no doubt have met a person who is so impressed with hearing himself talk that he continually dominates every conversation. But does he have something of value to say? Are you not more impressed with the person who speaks less often but makes a worthwhile contribution when he does say something? So it is in business writing. A letter that rambles on and on, and says nothing, loses the interest of its reader and certainly does not consider the situation from the reader's point of view. Remember, the reader is busy and his time costs money.

You should not "slice" a message to the point that it is incomplete; this is an expensive word-saving tactic. Learn to pack your message with complete ideas expressed in as few words as possible.

One of the best ways for you to master the skill of being concise, but not to the point of being incomplete, is to check the average length of your sentences. Writers in business should naturally aim at variety in both length and pattern of sentences. Research indicates that sentences of 15 to 20 words in length have the highest readability. Naturally, you will have some sentences that will be as short as 10 words or less and some that will be as long as 30 words. If you will make it a practice to check the average length of sentences, however, you will critically evaluate long sentences by weighing each word as to its relevance to an idea or thought. Is this not once again considering the situation from the reader's point of view? The busy reader will be annoyed with monotonous, wordy messages that could have been "sliced to be concise."

Such wordy and monotonous messages reflect the "gobbledy-gook" tendency of many of the verbal and written communications of our day. The movie *War on Gobbledygook,* filmed by the OFM Productions, points out the gobbledygook of sight and sound, with special emphasis on writing. Since the opposite of gobbledygook is simplicity, directness, and honesty in choice of words, you should attempt to ration your words and eliminate clutter from your business writing. The following excerpts are examples of gobbledygook revised to be "short and sweet, yet vivid and complete."

GOBBLEDYGOOK

Permit me to take this opportunity to thank you for your letter of January 2, which I have just received, for your kind comments about our Advertising Manual, and for your request for a copy of the Advertising Manual. We are flattered by the fact that you and many other people have liked it so much. In reply I wish to state that I wish it were possible to send you a copy of the manual with my compliments, free of any charge. I am compelled to say, however, that the fact is that requests for copies of the manual have been so numerous that it has become necessary that we now have to charge $1 for each copy of the manual.

In accordance with our new policy, will you please send us your check or money order for $1, and as soon as we receive your $1, we shall mail you a copy of the manual as soon as possible. May I say that because of the fact that the printer has not filled our last order for more copies of the manual, there may be a short delay in mailing your copy of the manual, but we shall do our best to send it as soon as possible.

In addition, please permit me to state that in the future we shall always be glad to answer any questions you may have about our advertising program. Let me assure you that we want you to call on us whenever there is something we can do for you. Needless to say, we, of course, shall welcome any suggestions you might wish to make for improving our Advertising Manual in the future.

SHORT AND SWEET, YET COMPLETE

Thank you for your comments about our Advertising Manual. Requests for copies have been so numerous it is necessary to charge $1 for each copy.

Upon receipt of your $1, we shall mail you a copy of the manual. Because the printer has not filled our last order for more copies, there may be a short delay until January 15.

Please feel free to call on us whenever there is something we can do for you and your advertising program. We welcome suggestions for improving our Advertising Manual in the future.

The last illustration gives a good example of *slicing* necessary words and phrases without distorting the meaning of the message. It would be unwise to slice this message any further, for overcutting may destroy clearness.

Consider the following letter written by a supposedly successful insurance company.

Dear Mr. Snyder:

Mrs. Carson has called to my attention your question regarding the amended fact sheet with respect to the recent increase in benefits for your group.

The statement "Any claim for benefits under this policy, which had its cause, origin, or beginning prior to the above date will be compensated in accordance with the benefits prior to the amendment date" may be a little confusing; however, I'm glad to clarify it. We administer claims on the basis of hospital confinement. We do not strictly administer on the cause, origin, or beginning basis. Rather, we look at a particular hospital confinement and see when the hospital confinement commenced, not when the condition which precipitated the hospital confinement commenced. If a man who has a chronic condition and if he was not confined, but at work on the effective date of the increase, is confined after that date, even though the condition commenced before the effective date of the increase, he will be paid on the basis of the increased benefit. This is the manner in which our Claims Department administers claims under this statement.

We're sorry for any unnecessary concern. Mr. Snyder, I hope I have satisfactorily clarified the matter for you, but should there be further question, just let me know.

Sincerely yours,

As the recipient of such an example of gobbledygook, consider how much more appreciative you would be if the message had been written to read:

Mrs. Carson has asked me to answer your questions regarding the increase in benefits for your group as stated on the amended fact sheet sent to you on June 12. The changes indicated are that claims on or after June 15 will be paid from the date that hospital confinement began rather than from the date that the illness began.

For example, if a man has a chronic illness but is not confined to a hospital until June 15 or after, he is eligible to receive the increased benefits when hospital confinement begins even though his chronic illness began before June 15.

Please feel free to contact me if you have any other questions regarding your policy.

Picture Perfect

Another way to achieve conciseness is to vividly and sharply portray a perfect picture in the reader's mind of the idea you are trying to convey. Developing this quality in your writing will give your message concreteness. A phrase such as "crisp, juicy, mouth-watering apples" captures a more vivid picture for the reader than the longer and more monotonous "good-eating apples of outstanding quality and flavor." The picture-evoking phrase gets the idea across in fewer words and with more meaning.

You will develop concreteness, or descriptive force, by using a good choice of nouns, adjectives, adverbs, and verbs which appeal to the five senses of seeing, hearing, touching, smelling, and tasting.

Colorless	*Concrete*
Intelligent student	Sharp as a tack
Very slender	Thin as a rail
Cold Icy Cola	Thirst-quenching Icy Cola
Very smooth	Smooth as velvet
Very quiet	Quiet as a mouse

Notice the pictorial zest of the concrete examples as contrasted to the bland, colorless, and unimaginative examples.

Another way to perfect the picture of your message is to be specific and definite so that your reader will have no difficulty knowing exactly what you want. To apply for "the position you advertised" is vague and elusive. To apply for "the clerk-typist position in your payroll department" is concrete and definite enough so that the reader immediately pictures the exact position you are applying for.

We received your letter of last week	Your letter of July 12
Your recent check in the amount of	Your May 10 check for $65
This morning we got your order for	Your order for
Leave to your choice the selection of	Choose
The new furniture you purchased	The octagonal cherrywood end table you purchased
We will mail your order soon	Your order will be mailed on June 10
The television you ordered	Your 25-inch Mercury portable, Model 2606

Notice how the specific and concrete examples have revitalized the vague and elusive ones.

"Get up, speak up, shut up, and sit down," the unofficial motto of the Toastmasters International, are words of wisdom to the business writer as well as the business speaker. This motto vividly portrays the message of "slice to be concise."

Examine the wordy and unclear message which follows:

We are sorry to tell you of the omission of the base from the package containing our new lamp shipped on May 10. We don't know how such a thing could have happened, and we are disgusted because we couldn't use the lamp for the party we held for our neighbors. We want a new one and soon.

Notice how clear, courteous, and to the point the same message can sound.

Will you please pick up and replace the lamp you delivered on May 10. Since the base is missing, we are unable to use it.

Rewrite the following slow, colorless letter on a sheet of paper. Colorless and wordy letters are deadly. They never make you like the writer or wish to meet him personally. The writer just does not seem pleased to be of service.

Dear Mr. Bein:

We are today in receipt of your letter of January 16, asking us to rush by air express the first item on your Order No. 785 which you placed for March 1 shipment. On investigation, we find that the complete order, including the other items, is packed and ready to be shipped. Therefore, instead of separating it, we are sending it as originally specified. With reference to your request for another copy of our spring catalog, we are sending one to you under separate cover.

Sincerely yours,

Does your letter get to the point, and reflect appreciation, the "you" attitude, and a "pleased to be of service" image like the following:

Thank you for your Order No. 785. You will be pleased to know that all the items you requested were available; therefore, the complete order was mailed air express today.

Your copy of our spring catalog, *Fashions Spring 1971*, has also been mailed to you for your early spring selections.

7

It's All in How You Say It

Tone It Up

"It's not always what you say—it's how you say it," and in no other case will this adage be more true than in business letter writing. Yes, indeed, how you "tone up" your writing or "how you say it" expresses your personality and that of any company or organization you may represent. Your friendly nature, your helpful manner, your radiant personality, and your courteous gestures must be reflected through the *positive tone* of your messages. Since we have already discussed and realized the importance of the "you" attitude and the reader's point of view, we have laid the groundwork necessary in developing the appropriate tone.

Mastering the development of the "you" attitude will naturally ensure that your messages are sincere, courteous, direct, and honest rather than sharp, blunt, overbearing, and pompous. Pleasant, persuasive, and convincing messages can only be realized if the reader's point of view has been foremost in your mind and in your writing.

Basically, your business writing will be of two types: (1) writing to arouse interest or to move to action and (2) writing to give information or knowledge.

Writing to arouse interest or to move to action is characteristic of sales letters, collection letters, and application letters, to mention a few. The *tone* of these letters must be persuasive, vivid, and convincing; therefore, they must appeal to basic wants and emotions.

The sales letter and the collection letter illustrated here are examples of letters stimulating interest and action.

Sales Letter

Dear TEEN MAIL Reader:

Why are so many young adults like yourself joining the swing to SUPER, the magazine for today's sophisticated teens?

It's simple—we know modern teens have a wide range of interests, and we try to keep you posted on all of them. But we don't tell you what to do. We just present the latest facts, the newest happenings . . . and let you make up your own mind!

SUPER is lively, colorful, exciting. And now, *exclusively for* TEEN MAIL *readers,* you can have it sent to you personally at HALF PRICE.

See for yourself why the smart set is swinging over to SUPER. Get 18 big issues (a full year and a half) for *only $3.00!* Detach and mail the postpaid card today—we'll bill you later.

Collection Letter

Dear Mr. Fowler:

Your account shows a balance due of $52.45 for children's clothing purchased during January and February.

This is the time of year when we must settle our accounts with our clothing houses, and we need every penny we can get our hands on.

Won't you pay up so that we can meet our commitments?

A stamped, addressed envelope is enclosed for your convenience in mailing us your check for $52.45.

Sincerely,

Notice how the vivid words of the sales letter—*young adults, swinging, sophisticated, lively, colorful, exciting, smart set*—have built an emotional appeal to teen-agers based on the lure of social approval by the "swinging set." Notice how the persuasive words of the collection letter—*need every penny we can get our hands on, pay up, meet our commitments*—also have built a moving plea based on the emotional appeal of "fair play."

Writing to give information or knowledge is characteristic of business summaries, office memoranda, statistical reports, minutes of meetings, and news releases. There may be occasion for you to give out such information. Remember that arousing interest and persuading to action are not predominant in these business communications, because they are usually assured. This type of writing must be accurate, complete, and exact.

The memorandum illustrated here is an example of writing to give information or knowledge.

Memorandum

TO: Diversified Vocational Clubs
FROM: Robert Smith, Executive Secretary
           Minnesota Diversified Vocational Clubs
DATE: August 17, 19—
SUBJECT: Organizational Packets for 19——19—

With this organizational packet, we launch our 19——19— year. Enclosed are some of National DVC's latest publications and a form you may use to order other publications or additional copies of the ones enclosed.

Important dates and activities that you should have on your calender are as follows:

National Membership Week
October 19–25, 19—

During this week, DVC members all over the nation will be working to reach 100 percent of their potential. Enclosed in this packet is information you will find very useful in a successful membership drive.

Membership Applications Due
October 30, 19—

Most states have set October 31 as the deadline for established clubs to submit membership applications in order that members may receive all the benefits of state and national membership. Organize as soon as the school year begins.

National DVC Week
March 8–14, 19—

In keeping with the recommendation of the National Program of Work Committee, the first national DVC Week will be held this year. You should include this as one of your outstanding activities during this school year. Watch for more information in the DVC Magazine.

Notice how the clear, direct, and explanatory words of the memorandum have built a message based on a matter-of-fact tone.

Accent the Positive—Eliminate the Negative

One of the best ways to "tone up" your letters is to accent the positive or pleasant and eliminate the negative or unpleasant. Consider some of your own acquaintances: "Bill is a pessimist —a real crybaby. Everybody is against him. Nothing ever goes right for him." On the other hand: "Charlie is an optimist. He is cheerful, positive, and happy to be alive." Whom would you rather be with, Bill or Charlie?

Your reader is even more critical of the company he keeps. He will avoid the pessimists—the negative and unpleasant letters—and will seek out the optimists—the positive and pleasant letters. Positive language stresses the light rather than the dark side. Positive language emphasizes what can be done and leaves what cannot be done to implication.

Observe how the following pessimistic or negative sentences

reveal an unpleasant tone. Then notice how the tone is improved in the optimistic or positive comparisons.

Negative	*Positive*
We are sorry but we cannot extend to you a speaker for $50.	You can have a first-class speaker for an honorarium of $100.
You failed to state what size you wanted; therefore we cannot send you the shoes.	You will receive your Scarpa shoes within three days if you send us your shoe size on the enclosed card today.
No deliveries will be made on Saturdays.	Deliveries are made Monday through Friday only.
We cannot pay for our hospital bill in one lump sum.	If you will accept $20 a month, we can clear up the balance in six months.

The disagreeable tone of *sorry, failed, no, cannot* is negative and unpleasant. The examples on the right indicate a more positive tone. It will be easier for you to communicate positiveness in your business letter writing if you are a positive person. However, if the message to be conveyed is negative, it becomes more difficult to keep the tone positive. The use of limiting words such as *only* and *exclusively*, and the use of conditional words such as *if* and *would*, can often produce a positive effect from a negative situation.

Goodwill is an intangible quality extremely important to the business letter writer. If he wants goodwill from others, he must give goodwill to them. You, as a writer, must convey the intangible quality of goodwill in your writing. You, as a writer, must, even under the most negative circumstances, convey the message that "the reader is always right." Isn't this once again considering the situation from the reader's point of view?

Consider the following negative letter. How would you improve the tone of this message?

Dear Mrs. Carson:

I was very disappointed and angry to have the raisins in my cake mix sink to the bottom. It was especially infuriating because my bridge club had no dessert because of your rotten product.

Don't you think you owe me an apology and money for a defective product?

Would you have written the letter in the more positive manner that follows? Perhaps the recipient of this letter would be more inclined to "do right by you" if you had.

Dear Mrs. Carson:

You will, I am sure, want to know that the raisins in your Streusel Coffee Cake Mix sink to and settle at the bottom of the cake when baked.

Will you please inform me if you feel I did not follow directions. Perhaps my supplier kept the mixes on the store shelves longer than feasible. Whatever the reason, I want to know so that I can once more restore my faith in Streusel Mixes, a family favorite of ours.

Sincerely yours,

8

A Powerful Takeoff ... a Smooth Landing

A "powerful takeoff" and a "smooth landing" are necessary to the most important parts of the letter—the first and the last paragraphs. Just as the pilot of a Boeing 747 needs power to get off the ground, you, as a letter writer, also need a powerful and forceful takeoff to get your letter off the ground.

Every writer likes to think that his message will absorb his reader's attention, but this is not always true. If you assume that the reader is a busy person having many claims on his attention, you'll realize you need strategy to capture a part of that attention. Unless you want your communication to receive the classification "junk mail," you must powerfully and forcefully come to the point in your first paragraph. You must, from your first word, have something to say. After you have said it, you should end your letter. Just as the pilot brings his plane in for a smooth landing at the completion of the flight, you must land your message smoothly at the completion of your thoughts.

The Takeoff

The "takeoff" or the first paragraph—and preferably the first sentence—should perform four important functions:

1. It should tell what the letter is about.
2. It should show courtesy and friendliness.
3. It should refer to any previous correspondence and sometimes to the date of that correspondence.
4. It should attempt to get favorable interest or action.

If your takeoff is powerful and forceful and direct and interesting, your letter may be read carefully. A good way to ensure this attention is to open with a short, strong, definite, action-getting statement. Make your opening short and make it say something. Why not consider your first sentence or your first short paragraph your headline. Don't be afraid to have only two or three short sentences in this first paragraph. Actually, the fewer the better. Unless the letter is a sales letter, the first paragraph must tell the reader what the letter is about. In a sales letter the first paragraph may appropriately be designed primarily to attract attention.

Remember that any reference to the date or details of previous correspondence should be placed in a subordinate position. In other words, "This communication is in reference to your letter of January 12" places the date of the previous correspondence in a predominant position; "Thank you for your letter of January 12 requesting 12 reams of our No. 16 white mimeograph paper" places the *thank you* and the actual order in a dominant position, with the date subordinate.

You will ensure a powerful takeoff if you can provide action in favor of your reader. This is always the most effective opening to a business communication. Action implies decision, and all of us are favorably impressed when our requests have been met. Notice in the following examples how action in favor of the reader gets the messages "off the ground."

Dear Mrs. Bennet:

Enclosed is our book, *Cooking With Spices,* which you requested in your letter of June 12. You will be pleased to know that this book is free of charge to all regular *Horizons* subscribers.

Dear Mr. Ellis:

Thank you for inquiring about the possibility of becoming our door-to-door salesman in the Midwest. Every one of us in the Minneapolis office feels that you would make an excellent addition to our marketing team.

Another way to ensure strength and power in your opening sentence or paragraph is to avoid the use of participial expressions. Such expressions indicate that the writer is having difficulty coming to the point and seems to be stalling. Inexperienced writers will encounter another problem with frequent use of participial expressions. Such expressions often force the writer to get into a bind that produces grammatically incorrect sentences. Notice how easily the following lengthy participial expression could be considered a complete sentence: "Having reviewed your application for employment as a secretarial trainee."

Avoid all unnecessary preliminaries in your first sentence and don't rehash what your reader already knows. For example, "Your order of January 10 reached my desk today" is obviously unnecessary and irrelevant. The reader realizes that his correspondence must have reached you or you would not be responding—so why rehash?

Remember that the first sentence and the first paragraph are extremely important. Everything that follows builds from this opening. Be natural and be yourself. It is a common practice for many writers to begin their first paragraph with the old-fashioned, pompous wordiness of yesteryear. Compare the following examples:

Yesteryear

We desire herewith to acknowledge receipt of your letter of June 10. Hereafter, in the future, we wish to inform you that it will be unnecessary for you to notify us directly. From this instant it is with pleasure that we announce that notification of late payments may be made to the respective agent in your city.

Now

Thank you for your letter of June 10 notifying us of late payment. All future notifications of late payments may be made directly to your agent, Mr. T. Jones.

Obviously, the natural, up-to-date version is easier to read as well as easier to write. The first message is wasteful and dates the writer. This example of yesteryear brings to mind the ancient characters in the days of Ebenezer Scrooge. Acting natural and saying things as you would when conversing with a friend is another way to get you off the ground with a powerful takeoff.

The Landing

The "landing," or the last paragraph of your letter, should have a definite purpose too. It should make it as easy as possible for the reader to take an action or to accept what the writer has written. If you have considered the reader's point of view from the first word of your letter to the last, you will show the reader how easy it is for him to do that which will benefit him. By enclosing an addressed envelope or postal card, you may readily stimulate action.

Probably the most serious error that a writer makes is to ramble, and the last paragraph seems to be the best place for such rambling. Beginning writers are sometimes perplexed and at a loss as to what would be an effective ending. If your message has been conveyed, make a smooth landing and end your letter. The reader doesn't expect you to be flowery or chatty. He doesn't expect and he doesn't want you to end your letter with the almost infamous "A speedy reply will be appreciated."

The most ineffective of all closings is the participial ending. It is weak and inconsequential. Ending your letter with "Trusting we shall hear from you soon" is as bad as beginning your letter with "Referring to your letter of June 10." Once again, remember that thanking in advance violates two rules of good letter writing. First, it is a participial expression; second, it is presumptuous and fails to give the reader the prerogative of decision.

You, as a writer, should remember that the last sentence should do three important things:

1. It should reflect courtesy.
2. It should summarize the message.
3. It should state the action desired.

Compare the "rough landings" illustrated on the left to the "smooth landings" on the right.

Rough Landing	*Smooth Landing*
Looking forward to hearing from you soon, we are	May we hear from you soon.
Hoping that you will fill my request soon	Enclosed is a self-addressed envelope for ease in mailing me the pamphlet.
Trusting you will give this matter your immediate consideration	Will you please act promptly on this request.

The pilot who makes a powerful takeoff and a smooth landing has largely ensured a pleasant flight for his passengers. You, the writer, with a powerful takeoff (a good opening paragraph) and a smooth landing (an effective closing paragraph), will almost guarantee your reader a pleasant journey through your message.

Compare the following ineffective opening sentences with their more effective counterparts. Which have more appeal to you?

1a. In regard to the furniture, it is being shipped from St. Paul today addressed to you at your home and have somebody there to receive the shipment because it must be signed for and will you be sure to acknowledge by letter to me.

1b. Will someone be at home to receive and sign for your new sofa and chair on January 10? Then if you will write to me, I will know they were satisfactory.

2a. In reply to your letter of July 1, I wish to advise you that an examination of my records shows that my policy is still in force.

2b. My records show that my policy is still in force.

3a. Acknowledging receipt of your letter of January 10 in which you asked for a copy of my cancelled check. I am glad to send you this copy.

3b. Enclosed is a copy of my cancelled check in full payment of my November statement.

4a. Referring to your letter of April 2, I want to tell you that I find your new publication extremely interesting.

4b. Thank you for mailing me a copy of your interesting booklet "Up, Up, and Away" on April 2.

5a. We desire herewith to acknowledge receipt of your esteemed favor on the 16th inst. We have given you credit for $69, the amount of the check enclosed.

5b. Your check mailed on May 16 for $69 has been credited to your account.

6a. With reference to your letter of June 12, I will be unable to attend your party.

6b. Thank you for inviting me to your party on Saturday, June 23. David and I are leaving for San Francisco on Friday, June 22. If we were going to be in town, nothing would prevent us from attending a Blackstone get-together.

Compare the following ineffective closing sentences with their counterparts. Which would you consider smoother landings?

1a. If you will send me a big order right away, it will help me win a prize in the contest that our club is conducting and you will receive merchandise that is superior in quality at no higher price than you have been paying at cosmetic counters in regular retail stores.

1b. If you will order more than ten bottles of Avantee Milk Bath today, it will allow you to give each of your regular customers a 20 per cent discount. Also, your order will help the Eastern region to win the sales award for 19__.

2a. Hoping it will be possible for me to give you my decision on this matter by Friday, we are,

2b. You will have my decision by Friday, June 10.

3a. Assuring you in advance of my appreciation for your kind attention and hoping that I may have the opportunity to do the same.

3b. Will you please allow me an interview? I would like to discuss my qualifications in person.

4a. Hoping you will accept these broken glasses for credit as soon as possible.

4b. Please credit my account for $22.95 for the broken glasses which were not accepted when delivered.

5a. Believing that you will find this explanation suitable, we beg to remain,

5b. If you wish further information regarding the return of the copperware, feel free to write to me again.

6a. With best regards, I remain,

6b. Best wishes for an exciting holiday.

Now consider the following three sentences and select the one that makes the best reference to the date of your reader's letter.

1. This is in reply to your letter, dated April 22.

2. Thank you for your interest in our advertising program, expressed in your letter of April 22.

3. We are in receipt of your letter of April 22.

If you selected the second sentence, you were correct. In this sentence the date is placed in a subordinate position; the "thank you" and "interest in our advertising program" are placed in a dominant position.

9

Simply Ask, Answer, and Appreciate

You may be sure that you will have many occasions to write routine letters of request, reply, and thank you. Although such letters are routine, you should not allow this everyday quality to minimize their importance. Every letter should make a good impression. After all, the letter is "you" to the reader. Every letter should reflect the "you" attitude. Every letter should be characterized by good structural units of thought which are organized, coherent, and forceful. Every letter should be concise and concrete.

Ask and You Will Receive

Letters of request are "asking" letters. You might ask for reservations; you might ask for literature, such as price lists, pamphlets, or articles; or you might ask for general or specific information. No matter what your letter requests, the most important characteristic it must possess is that it be specific. To violate this consideration is a serious mistake. If the recipient of your request must write you to ask for more specific information, you are violating the rule of courtesy, the "you" attitude, and you are by no means considering the situation from the reader's point of view. It is important, then, that your message be worded simply, completely, forcefully, and courteously.

It will be to your advantage if when feasible you enclose a stamped, addressed envelope so as to make your request easy to meet. It is also essential to include a return address on the letter itself. This rule of courtesy is often violated, especially when the request is of a personal nature and a letterhead is not used. Are you considering the situation from the reader's point of view if you force him to file the soiled envelope along with the letter, in order to have your address available?

The letters of request that will be discussed in this section are hotel reservations, literature requests, letters that request general or specific information, and personal requests and invitations. All of these letters may be very brief. Each should, in the first sentence, state the request and, when applicable, state why this request is being made of this particular recipient. Then each should give whatever details are necessary to enable the reader to fully understand the request. The letter should end courteously, but remember, do not *thank in advance*.

Is There Room in the Inn?

The following example of a routine request for a hotel reservation is brief, but complete. Although it is not always essential, information such as preference of room or location may be included.

Will you please reserve a single room with shower for me for Saturday, January 21. Because of a late flight, I expect to check in about midnight. Please confirm this reservation before January 15.

Literature, Please!

The request for literature is usually not as brief as a reservation letter. Whenever possible, address your request to a particular individual. Sometimes, doing so may require extra effort on your part and may even necessitate a local telephone call to the company involved. If it is impractical to obtain this information, at least write to the specific department that will handle your request. For example, if you are asking for a salary schedule from a particular firm, you should write to the personnel department; if you are asking for advertising literature, you should write to the advertising department. When making a request, be sure you have a clear picture in your mind as to what you want, and convey this same clear picture to your reader.

Even though this letter is a routine letter of request, you should remember to maintain a good "you" attitude. It will not be difficult for you to change "I want 75 copies" to "Will you please send 75 copies." Make sure that the literature you request is not published for public sale and sold by a publishing company. Your resourcefulness in this matter will save your reader time and will save you possible embarrassment.

It is courteous and shows good common sense to indicate how you intend to reimburse your reader for any production or mailing costs involved. It is presumptuous to request several copies without assuming some cost. If only one copy of a pamphlet or other item is requested, a stamped, addressed envelope may sufficiently cover the mailing cost.

The following is an example of a concise, complete, and concrete request for literature:

Will you please send us a copy of your free pamphlet *Ahead of the Game*, published in June, 19__. Everyone I know in advertising seems to be singing the praises of your advertising brochure.

Since I am attending an advertising forum on March 15–16 in Denver, and want to read it before I leave, will you please mail it to me before March 14 in the enclosed stamped, addressed envelope.

Information, Please!

The letter requesting general or specific information will vary depending upon the information requested. Of course, it should have the characteristics of a good "you" attitude, conciseness, completeness, and concreteness. If the letter deals with more than one question, you may wish to treat each question as a separate paragraph.

In the following example, a writer is making inquiry to a postage meter company:

Will you please answer the following questions regarding the purchase of a postage meter machine for my secretarial service business which I operate in my home. I have a monthly volume of 200 letters.

Please inform me as to the advantage of buying versus renting a postage meter machine.

How about the cost? Would it be feasible for a small business such as mine to invest in such a machine?

Since I am planning to use my envelopes as an advertising medium, I would prefer a machine that can stamp the postage and advertisement in one operation. Will your machine print both an advertisement and a stamp?

The Easy-Seal machine will seal envelopes as well as print postage. Will your machine also perform both of these operations?

A better way to request information which deals with more than one question is to enumerate your questions. Each of the enumerations should be a separate paragraph. As you can see in the following example, this method keeps the inquiry clear and brief and enables the recipient to organize his answers.

Will you please answer the following questions regarding the use of a postage meter machine for my small secretarial service business which I operate in my home. I have a monthly volume of 200 letters.

1. Would I be better off to buy or rent this machine?
2. How much does one cost?
3. Does this small machine print an advertisement?
4. Does this machine seal envelopes?

End this letter courteously and avoid the trite, stereotyped expression "We shall appreciate receiving your reply as soon as possible." It is quite obvious to the reader that if you spent the time and effort to request information, you would be appreciative of his answer. "As soon as possible," in this instance, is also an example of the lack of concreteness. If you have a definite deadline, state it; otherwise, assume that the reader will give your request prompt attention.

Following is an example of a good letter requesting information:

Will you please send me the name, address, and telephone number of your salesman for the Roseville area? Roseville is a suburb of St. Paul, located 30 miles from the central city.

Since I have just moved to Minnesota from New Jersey and have always used Avantee Cosmetics, I want to contact the salesman immediately.

A stamped, addressed postcard is enclosed for your reply.

The following examples of request letters are not demanding. They are short, to the point, and yet courteous. Would you grant requests made like these?

Hotel Reservation

Gentlemen:

Please reserve a room for me, John Freeman, vice-president of Wheeler Laboratories, 1214 East Aquila Street, Hartford, Connecticut 06118, for Friday, June 11. I will arrive at 8:30 p.m.; therefore, please hold the room for my late arrival.

I prefer a first-floor room with a shower, double bed, and color television.

Will you please confirm this reservation and inform me if you will be able to accommodate my specific requests.

Requesting a Contribution

Dear Mr. Edwards:

Each year at this time your firm is generous in its financial contribution to the New Hope Home for Girls.

You of all people, Mr. Edwards, are aware of the good work that the Home does for the young girls in our community. Perhaps you have not heard, however, that plans are now under way to expand the gymnasium. Its present size is not large enough for competitive sports.

Enclosed is a pledge for $1,000, the amount that Carter & Sons regularly subscribes. You know it will be put to good use immediately.

Literature Request

Enclosed is my check for $3.88 for a one-year, special-offer subscription to *Better Living*. Please send the magazine to me at my home address, which is given in the return address of this letter.

Request to Temporarily Cancel Delivery Service

Will you please cancel mail delivery service to my home effective Monday, June 21, 19__, to Monday, July 21, 19__.

Since I will be out of town and on vacation during that time, will you please hold mail at the post office until my return on the 21st.

An Informal Invitation (handwritten)

Will you join us for cocktails? We are celebrating the publication of Lucille Ananson's book of poems, *Living Poems*, from 4:00 to 6:00 p.m. on Saturday, February 17, 19__, at the home of the Roger Smiths, 13 Pepperidge Drive, Morristown, New Jersey.

A map is enclosed to help you find your way.

Fold-over Card—Informal Invitation (handwritten)

Dear Bertha,

Will you and John join us for brunch at eleven o'clock on Sunday, January 24?

Love, Valerie

A Formal Invitation (either engraved or handwritten messages are preferred)

Mr. and Mrs. David Evans
request the honor of your presence
at a reception
in honor of
Professor Lucille Ananson
celebrating the publication of her book
LIVING POEMS
on Saturday, February 17
from four-thirty to six-thirty o'clock
Catskill Room
Hotel James
Six Speedwell Avenue
Morristown

Formal Business Invitation (engraved or printed)

Mr. Donald L. Ferris
Vice President
Dow-Smith Book Company
cordially invites you to a
Cocktail Reception
for Dow-Smith authors
on Thursday evening, February twenty-fifth
Nineteen hundred and seventy-one
from half past five to half past six o'clock
at the Buckingham Room, Main Floor South
of the Pick-Congress Hotel
Michigan Boulevard and Congress Parkway
Chicago, Illinois

Husbands and wives
are invited to attend.

Invitation to an Official Dinner (engraved or printed)

Mr. and Mrs. Jonathan Bly, Jr.
request the pleasure of your company
at a dinner in honor of
The Honorable Senator of New Jersey
Frederick Van Appleton
and
Mrs. Marion Van Appleton
Sunday, the eighteenth of March
at eight o'clock
Empire Room of the Waldorf-Astoria

R.S.V.P.   Black Tie
245 Park Avenue
New York City

Engraved Invitation to a Formal Dinner

Mr. and Mrs. Donald Gross
request the pleasure of your company
at dinner
on Saturday, June the twentieth
at eight o'clock
230 Morris Avenue

R.S.V.P.

Handwritten Invitation to a Formal Dinner

Mr. and Mrs. Donald Gross
request the pleasure of
Mr. and Mrs. George Smith's
company at dinner
on Saturday, June the twentieth
at eight o'clock

R.S.V.P.   Butterworth Farms
                                            Morristown, New Jersey

General Information Request

Will you please tell me how to enroll for adult evening classes at the
Dover High School.

Since I have been out of high school for ten years, I wish to regain
some of my shorthand and typewriting skills, and update myself regarding office procedures. I want to re-enter the office-occupations
work force as soon as I am prepared.

Perhaps you have a descriptive course catalog that would be helpful in my selection of classes.

Promptly We Reply

You will be answering request letters as well as writing them. The most important rule to follow in handling replies is to answer *promptly*. When giving information, be exact and brief. If a request is made in the form of paragraphs, answer in the form of paragraphs. If a request is made in the form of enumerations, answer in the form of enumerations. The following example is a reply to the letter of inquiry on page 57:

Thank you for your interest in our Randolph Speedy Mailer. You will enjoy reading the enclosed brochure, which describes the mailer in detail.

It is to your advantage to purchase the Speedy Mailer on a rental-purchase plan. This allows you to make rental payments with an option to buy.

As indicated in the enclosed brochure, businesses with a monthly volume of 200 letters "sing the praises" of the Speedy Mailer.

The cost of the meter depends on the amount of postage used, as outlined on page 6 of the brochure.

You will be pleased to know that the Speedy Mailer prints advertisements and stamps the envelopes in one simple operation (see page 8). It also seals the envelopes with ease and speed (see page 9).

OR

Thank you for your interest in our Randolph Speedy Mailer. You will enjoy reading the enclosed brochure, which describes the mailer and answers your questions in detail.

1. It would be to your advantage to rent the Speedy Mailer with an option to buy.

2. The cost of the meter is proportionate to the amount of postage used (see page 6).

3. The Speedy Mailer seals envelopes and prints advertisements and stamps in one simple operation (see pages 8–9).

Since the letter of reply should possess qualities that will create goodwill—just as every piece of business correspondence should—the most courteous reply is one that gives favorable action. This letter is the easiest to write because, after a brief thank you for the request, a positive statement is made giving information, answering the questions, or indicating the pamphlet will be mailed.

The more difficult letter to write is the one that does not grant the request or can only partially grant the request. Even though you do not have all the answers, all the figures, or all the data, you can always make some positive suggestion or give some help. Remember to accent the positive information by stating it first, and then follow it with reasons why the complete request cannot be met. For example:

Thank you for your order for a copy of our brochure *Ahead of the Game.*

One free copy was mailed to you on March 3.

Because of the popularity of this brochure, our supply is temporarily depleted. Additional copies are being printed now and will be available by March 15.

The letter of confirmation is very important in maintaining goodwill; therefore, all letters making requests should be acknowledged in writing. A letter should always accompany any piece of literature, check, or so on, thus allowing the sender to build goodwill as he promotes his product or service.

It is especially rude not to reply to requests. It is especially courteous and in good taste to reply to requests promptly. Your prompt reply indicates to the reader that you have given the matter immediate attention. This in itself is a compliment and considers the situation from the reader's point of view.

The following examples of letters of confirmation reflect the writer's ability to maintain goodwill. Remember, answering promptly is the first rule to follow.

Confirming a Reservation

Dear Mr. Freeman:

A beautiful, large, single room located on the first floor facing Merry Lane Park has been reserved for you for Friday, June 11, at the special rate of only $19.

Since you plan to arrive later than 7:00 p.m. we will, of course, hold your room for your 8:30 p.m. late arrival.

We certainly look forward to making your stay in New Orleans enjoyable again, Mr. Freeman.

Acknowledging Request for Literature

Thank you for your kind remarks about our brochure, *Getting Ahead*. A copy has been mailed to you today, free of charge.

If you need more than one brochure, please let us know. For additional copies, a small printing cost and mailing fee of 50 cents a copy is all that is necessary.

It is always courteous to acknowledge all letters of request; therefore, all invitations (both formal and informal) should be confirmed even if an R.S.V.P. notation has not been included. Many people feel that it is correct to reply only if one declines an invitation. This, of course, is not correct. All requests should be confirmed, preferably in the manner in which they were received. In other words, if the request was made by telephone, then a confirmation can be made in the same way, by telephone. However, if the request was made in writing, the reply should also be in writing.

Accepting a Formal Invitation (a handwritten message is preferred)

Mr. and Mrs. David Anderson
accept with pleasure
the kind invitation of
Mr. and Mrs. David Evans
on Saturday, February seventeenth
at four-thirty o'clock

Regret to a Formal Invitation (handwritten and answered in same degree of formality as the invitation)

Mr. and Mrs. David Anderson
regret
that because of their absence from town
they will be unable to accept
Mr. and Mrs. David Evans'
kind invitation for the seventeenth of February

Declining an Informal Invitation (handwritten messages are preferred)

Thank you for including Don and me in your plans to celebrate Lucille's first publishing venture with an open house at the Roger Smiths' on February 17.

If we had not promised the Essex High Ski Club that we would chaperone their Vermont ski trip that weekend, we would be there.

Since we cannot attend, please accept our best wishes for a fun time and extend our congratulations to Lucille.

Apologies for Declining a Personal Invitation (handwritten)

Dear Ann,

You will, I hope, receive this message in time to include another couple in your plans to attend the Army–Navy game. What a stroke of luck for Jack winning four tickets to the game of the year! Thank you for inviting us, you were most thoughtful.

Since my mother is flying in on Saturday, November 20, we will have to drive to Newark on that day to pick her up at the airport. Both David and I are disappointed that these two big occasions had to coincide.

Have a fun time and cheer Army to its second victory for us, too.

Cordially,

Much Obliged

Now is the time to say "thank you." When you have received a helpful reply to your letter of request, you are correct in writing a "much obliged" letter of appreciation to thank your correspondent. Of course, you realize the importance of saying "thank you" in verbal communications; it is no less important in written communications. If ever in doubt whether you should write a letter of thanks, write it. What can you lose? Goodwill? Simply say "thank you," and don't preface it with "I want to thank you." The *thank you* is the most "you" attitude phrase you can use. Why preface it with *I want to* and weaken the forcefulness of the "you" attitude?

Ending your letter with the trite and stereotyped "Thanks again" also weakens the effectiveness of your letter. It is redundant, as you have already said it in your first sentence. If you can honestly and sincerely state how the reply has helped you, do so and end your letter.

Thank You for the Literature

The following letter illustrates a brief but courteous "thank you":

Thank you for your informative and well-illustrated brochure *Getting Ahead of the Pack.*

The manner in which you have presented growth-on-the-job ideas has encouraged me to do something about my present job.

Thank You for the Autographed Picture

The following example is a pleasant, courteous "thank you" written by Florence Brown to John Lewis, promotion manager for the New York Mets. Mr. Lewis had promptly answered a request for an autographed team picture for her nephew's birthday. Florence's nephew was elated with the picture.

Thank you for the beautiful, colored, autographed picture of the New York Mets sent to me on June 10.

Because of your prompt reply, I received it in time to give it to my ten-year-old nephew, David, for his birthday party on June 12.

You can imagine the hit his uncle made when he presented him with the most treasured gift of all.

This next letter illustrates a nice way to say thank you to Midwestern Mills. They had promptly answered a request made by Josephine Credia for information regarding their Betty Cracker Kitchen Tours which are scheduled every Tuesday and Thursday at 10:15 a.m. and 2:15 p.m. How rude it would have been for Josephine not to say "much obliged" for the information requested, even though the ladies could not, as a group, take advantage of the tours.

Thank You for the Information

Thank you for your prompt reply to my letter of June 10 requesting information regarding your schedule for Betty Cracker Kitchen Tours.

Since the ladies in our group do volunteer work for Methodist Hospital every Tuesday and Thursday as Pink Ladies, we will be unable to take advantage of the tours as a group experience.

It is important to be especially friendly when writing a thank you for a personal gift. It must be sincere and courteous.

Thank You for the Personal Gift

Dear Jonathan,

Jonathan, you have always had a most uncanny ability to give the perfect gift that delights the recipient. The antique cameo was no exception. Thank you.

If you will come to dinner on Saturday, May 14, at 8:00 p.m., I shall wear it so that I can show you how elegant it looks when worn with one of my favorite dresses.

10

Handle with Care

Some requests require a "handle with care" warning. These letters are more of a challenge than the simple reservation, literature, or information requests discussed in Chapter 9. Since these letters are persuasive requests, you must treat them with special care. The importance of the "you" attitude is even more relevant, and whenever possible, appeals should be made to personal satisfaction and benefits to your reader.

Special Orders

The letter you write ordering goods or services without an order blank is a "handle with care" letter. It is special because it is a letter that you will not have to write often, as most ordering is done with carefully planned and constructed order blanks and requisition forms. These are nearly foolproof and should be used whenever possible; however, many goods and services are ordered by letter.

Ordering goods without an order blank is considered a special request and requires special handling. Letters asking special favors are also considered special-request letters. Most companies welcome such letters because they usually represent new customers and allow the company to build goodwill.

Ordering Without an Order Blank

After writing a special-order letter you should be able to answer yes to each of the following questions:

1. Was your order complete? Was it crystal clear what you wanted?
   a. Did you open with a definite request, such as "Please ship me the following," or did you hint as to what you wanted, like "I should like to have"?
   b. Did you include a complete description of the goods wanted? (Remember, you did not have a catalog or a price list.) Did you describe the goods completely and in a logical order, such as:
      Quantity
      Units (pounds, bushels, gross, dozens)
      Catalog number
      General description (brand or trade name)
      Specific details (color, style, size, weight)
      Unit and total price
   c. Did you carefully cover shipping instructions? If you have no special preference, did you specifically state "Ship the best way possible"?
      If you had a specific request, did you remember to include what carrier and what route?
      Since you needed the goods in a hurry, did you give a specific deadline?
   d. Did you remember to include terms of payment and type of remittance?
      If payment is the method customarily used, did you refer to it?

If you included the remittance, did you refer to the enclosed check?

If you wanted the amount added to your established account, did you indicate such a request?

2. Did you arrange and tabulate your letter so that the person handling the order could identify the items quickly and not overlook any?

a. Did you set up a table?

b. Did you single-space the description of each item?

c. Did you double-space between items?

d. Did you use abbreviations and symbols in describing the items?

e. Did you capitalize the first letter of the description?

f. Did you use leader lines to connect the items to prices?

3. Did you maintain a friendly, courteous tone? Were you as concise as possible?

The following special-order letter illustrates a form that has advantages of attractiveness, clarity, and completeness. As you will notice, sometimes much space is required to include such advantages.

Grand Typewriter Sales
140 Second Avenue South
Hopkins, MN 55343

Gentlemen:

Please rush the following items as listed in your 1970 catalog by parcel post by January 10:

2 doz.—Typewriter ribbons, black nylon, for
    standard Grand, @$1 . . . . $24.00
1 doz.—Typewriter ribbons, black, carbon,
    for Electric Grand, @$2 . . . . 24.00
1 box—Typewriter erasers, stik-a-pen, brush end,
    light green, @$.33 . . . . 8.25
                                TOTAL $56.25

You may bill the items and delivery charges to our regular monthly charge account.

                                       Sincerely yours,

Situations may arise in your personal life forcing you to order goods without an order blank. Remember to follow the same good writing procedures for these situations.

The following is an example of a neatly tabulated special-order letter. Notice how accurate, complete, clear, and concise the message is. Such an order is welcomed because it is so complete and clear.

Usually you expect prompt delivery of the goods and services you have ordered, but always remember, to insure speedy delivery, all order letters must include sufficient information.

Will you please mail me the following items from your *Rows' SPRING 1971* catalog, c.o.d.

Catalog No.	Quantity	Item	Color	Price
57F2204	1	AM Radio	Black	$ 5.59
57F3230	1	Phonograph	Red and White	14.75
6F70839	1	Air Mattress	Print	1.97
28F7514	1	Helmet	White	14.50
			Total.	$36.81

Please send these items by December 10, as they will be Christmas gifts for my niece and nephew.

Asking a Favor

A letter asking a favor is another special-request letter that requires special handling. By its very nature it involves people personally; therefore, it becomes precariously sensitive. If every favor that you asked or which was asked of you could be answered positively, this type of letter could be considered a routine request and would require little or no special handling; however, the letter that requests a favor must be written with extreme tact so that it will be given careful attention and consideration. You must prepare this letter in the most persuasive manner, so as to ensure a welcome reception.

In this letter, as in all the letters of request, it is imperative that you specifically and tactfully ask the favor early in the letter. Because your reader is curious, it is also a good idea to indicate why you have made this request of him. For example:

You have the reputation of being the top electric typewriter salesman in the country. Will you please allow an inexperienced distributive education student from the Detroit area to benefit from your knowledge?

I am writing a paper on direct selling and would appreciate any ideas you have regarding selling techniques.

After you have made your specific request, it is important that you explain your request so that it will be easy for your recipient to answer you. You may end this letter by restating the request and closing courteously.

Sometimes, in the effort to be courteous and tactful, a writer runs the risk of becoming negative. For example, "I know that you are an extremely busy man and that you probably get hundreds of requests like mine, but I am hoping you will give my request special consideration" is a negative approach that could easily encourage a negative answer. Cautiously avoid any suggestion to your reader that your favor will not be granted, that your reader is too busy, or that your request or suggestion could not possibly succeed.

Asking Assistance

Mary Bradwahl does a good job of requesting the advice of a highly paid secretary in her area in initiating a program of salary reviews for her firm.

Will you please help other secretaries in your area learn from your experience so that they might achieve the success and reputation that you have attained.

At 7 p.m. on Monday, May 13, the 25 secretaries in our firm are meeting at the Civic Center in Room 276 to discuss a program of salary reviews. Any information you can give us before that meeting (or, if time permits, at the meeting) would be valuable in initiating our program.

Consider the friendly, persuasive manner of the following special-request letter. The writer has made sure that he has given the reader enough information.

You have hired office-education cooperative part-time training students for all the years that our school has offered a program to its vocational students. On several occasions you have talked to me about the advantages of such a program.

Would you be interested in making a 40-minute presentation at the December 20 Chamber of Commerce luncheon at 11:30 a.m. at the Ambassador Motel?

Many employers are not familiar with the cooperative training program and have asked me to schedule a program which would familiarize them with such a program.

Let me know if you can make it. I will be happy to pick you up shortly after 11 a.m. for the December 20 monthly Chamber luncheon.

Friendly Persuasion Softens a Personal Complaint

The following is an example of a very special request letter because it asks the reader to take care of a personal nuisance. Notice how it handles with care a somewhat ticklish request that could cause hard feelings.

Dear Mrs. Edwards,

You will be surprised to hear that your friendly dog, Trojan, has been mischievous lately during his early morning runs. He has been upsetting the trash cans on Corn Hill and eating from them.

Frankly, Mrs. Edwards, I am afraid Trojan will eat something that will make him sick, with all the pesticides and things that people discard these days. Perhaps Trojan will have to be escorted during his run or confined to the yard until he breaks this habit.

In any event, he's a most handsome collie and his safety is of utmost importance. Kind regards to all of you.

Cordially,

11

Special Delivery

Just as the special-order letters require special handling, the replies to these special orders should also be handled with care. Probably the most commonly written reply will be one which acknowledges an order and tells the reader that the goods or services are on their way. This type of letter has one major goal —building goodwill. Like the letter granting a favor, it is positive and is pleasant to write. A reply letter which acknowledges an incomplete order or refuses a favor, because of its negative message, is more difficult to write.

All Right, All Ready

Obviously, the best thing to do is to fill the order immediately, or at least inform the person ordering when the order will be filled. Any time there is a delay, the buyer should be informed. The writer who attempts to be a public relations man in every letter he writes is keen enough to be aware that the letter that acknowledges an order can promote goodwill. As already stated, the letter that tells the buyer "all right, all ready"—your order is on its way—is positive and easy to write. However, it must accomplish certain things.

If the primary objective of a letter is to create goodwill, it will be the writer's goal to emphasize the things that will have high reader interest. For example, if the shipment can be made exactly to the reader's specifications, this news alone will be "good news" and should be told directly with enthusiasm. Less important things such as when the order was received, details of packing, and payment arrangements should be included, but in a subordinate position.

Consider the following three examples:

1. We were pleased to receive your order, and it will be shipped today.
2. Your order was shipped today, and you should receive it soon.
3. Your order (Invoice No. 236) should arrive on Tuesday, June 25, as we shipped it airmail today.

Do you agree that the third sentence is most reader-oriented?

If you selected the third example because you have considered the reader, you would probably give the following reason:

It gives specific information so that the reader is not left worrying and wondering when his order will arrive. Also, it is positive and will be accepted as good news.

Once you have enthusiastically given a quick opening, you may then proceed to handle the somewhat less significant details, such as the practical aspects of when the order was received and packing and payment arrangements. Perhaps the following example will clarify this discussion:

Your order for 20 cases of assorted Rosedale Farm Candies should reach you on Monday, as we shipped it by truck yesterday. You will be pleased to know that your Invoice No. 264 totaling $400 and delivery costs of $22.50 were charged to your regular charge account No. 411425, as you requested in your order of April 6.

Can you see how this illustration gets off to a good start and still brings in the practical details? You may question the fact that nothing has been said about thanking the writer for the order. It is not intended to ignore this excellent opportunity to be appreciative and grateful for the order or in some instances to welcome new accounts. It is important, however, to realize that this does not take priority over the good news of positive action. By all means allow yourself to be appreciative in the letter; however, do it after you have indicated action. Be careful to avoid such trite expressions as "Much obliged for your order" or "Welcome to our family of charge customers." Sometimes the tone of your letter will be the only thing necessary to indicate your appreciation.

Using the above example for your opening paragraph, complete the letter on a sheet of paper. Attempt to follow these suggestions: Show appreciation without being gushy, welcome your new customer, resell your product, and end your letter with a friendly comment so as to build goodwill.

Compare your letter with the following list and check any points you may have omitted:

1. Did the letter have a direct, reader-oriented beginning that covered ground fast? Did it avoid wishy-washy idle chatter like "We received your order and were happy to fill it"?

2. Did you take care of the practical details: order number, description of goods, invoice number, method of payment, packing details?

3. Did you attempt to sincerely develop goodwill by using a "you" attitude, thanking the writer for the order, welcoming a new customer, and closing with a friendly—but not trite—comment?

4. Did you attempt to resell your product and suggest profit-making, pricing, and other good sales-promotion ideas?

If your letter has included the items on the check list, you can be assured that it will receive an enthusiastic welcome and that you have handled this special order with care.

Very Interesting—but Stupid

Acknowledging a special order that is complete and specific with positive action is much easier and more pleasant than acknowledging an incomplete order. Your first reaction to an incomplete order will probably be "very interesting—but stupid," because you are perturbed by the inconvenience and delay caused by the writer's oversight. An implication of "very interesting—but stupid" in your reply, however, does not reflect a reader-oriented attitude. Your objective will be to minimize the unfortunate results of incomplete orders, avoid embarrassing the writer, and get the information needed to complete the order.

It is not necessary to trace the tragedy step by step; in fact, it probably does not have to be stated at all, merely implied. Apologizing for the inconvenience and delay will only depress the reader and accent the negative. Putting the reader on the spot by challenging his accuracy is antagonizing. Just as indefensible is the apologetic manner, blaming yourself for not being able to understand the order. Both of these approaches question the reader's intelligence. Your primary concern should be to get the information necessary to complete the order. This is the only way you can possibly attempt to handle this negative situation.

Since the acknowledgment of a vague-order letter is by its very nature negative, you should open the letter by making "friendly talk." Obviously the friendly talk should be about the products ordered. Remember, however, this chatty opening should be brief and sincere and should set the stage for the negative message. It is important to avoid using any negative words whatsoever. Probably the best opening you could choose would be that which makes reference to the desirability of the product. The opening should refer to the actual order and indicate appreciation for the order.

If you consider the situation from the reader's point of view, it will be easier for you to move from your introduction to the actual negative message. This emphasized "you" attitude will be your only chance to shift into the bad news without offending your reader.

Let's illustrate a chatty, friendly opening with a "you" attitude shift into the negative news, followed by a pleasant, positive closing.

Dear Miss Fredricks:

You will be thrilled with the modern, clean, general appearance of your correspondence when you use the variety of type-style elements available for your new Manning electric typewriter. Thank you for your October 15 c.o.d. parcel post order for four electric nickel-type elements.

So that you can get exactly the type style you wish, will you please review the enclosed pocketbook catalog and make a selection. If you will notice, we have marked in red those styles which have been the most popular.

After reviewing the catalog, will you please check your selections on the enclosed stamped, addressed order card and mail it to us today. Upon receipt of this card, we will mail your four electric type-style elements immediately, as all models are in stock.

Sincerely yours,

This example does a good job of holding off the bad news until the customer is in a good mood. The opening paragraph does a good job of cushioning the blow (no type-style elements for a while) and also restates the desirability of the product. The final, friendly note (making it easy for the reader to reply) is positive and not stereotyped, like "A stamped, addressed envelope is enclosed for your convenience."

Mrs. Charles Burba, a new customer from a small town fifty miles away, wants a bottle of Misty Lee spray cologne at $6 and three tubes of Misty Lee frosted lipstick at $3 each sent c.o.d. She has requested that you mail them today, so she will get them tomorrow. You advertised these prices with tax included. One problem—you have twenty-two shades of frosted lipstick from which she may select and she forgot to tell you what shade she wants. You're not a mind reader; you have plenty of lipstick in stock and you could fill the order if she had only told you the shade. On a sheet of paper, write a letter to get her choice of shade, to establish her as a new customer, and to persuade her to keep ordering.

Now check to make sure you did not include any of the following expressions in your letter to Mrs. Burba:

1. "Thank you for your order" (stereotyped, cold expressions should be avoided).

2. "We find that you did not include" or "We regret that we cannot serve you until you tell us just what you want" (negative expressions and words should be completely avoided).

3. "A card is enclosed for your convenience" (too shopworn; be more specific).

4. "Tell us what shade you want and we will ship the order" (lacks the goodwill effect and leaves the customer cold).

The following letter invites a prompt response. It encourages the reader to send the necessary information, as well as establishes her as a new customer.

You are going to enjoy your new Misty Lee spray cologne because of the improvement in the atomizer. Thank you for your c.o.d. parcel post order of October 12.

You will also be happy to know that Misty Lee now comes in 22 shades of frosted lipsticks—a selection never before offered. So that you may get exactly the shade that complements your complexion and apparel, check your three choices on the enclosed stamped, addressed card. As soon as we receive it, we will rush the cologne and lipsticks to you so that you may enjoy them early this spring.

Sure Thing

Letters granting favors are similar to letters acknowledging orders, in that both are positive. You will find it easy to say "Yes" or "Sure thing—happy to oblige." If you are asked to write a letter granting a special favor, such as accepting a speaking engagement or serving as a member of a panel, do so enthusiastically. Don't fall into an unplanned, stereotyped acceptance style like the one which follows:

I am pleased to have the opportunity to speak to your economics class as requested in your letter of November 1.

I have been in the banking business for almost 50 years and have a very good practical analysis of economics for everyday living.

I think I will give a talk on "Economics in Everyday Living" as I see it. If you wish, I could have some visual aids.

Thank you again. I consider it an honor and a privilege to be asked, and I will be there promptly at 9:05 a.m.

The preceding unplanned, stereotyped letter of acceptance indicates that if this man speaks like he writes, he will be a complete bore. Consider the following enthusiastic, favorable reply to this speaking invitation:

Thank you! With pleasure I accept your invitation to speak to your economics class.

Your students, like most young people, would probably like to hear practical application of economics to just plain everyday living. The slide presentation which I have used with high school students has been received enthusiastically because of its modern approach and up-to-date analysis. Can you provide me with a screen and a projector?

Tell your students I will be there at 9:05 in Room 232 next Friday morning and that I don't plan to put anybody to sleep.

The second letter shows a little life and does the following things:

1. Accepts graciously and immediately (this should please the reader or he wouldn't have extended the invitation in the first place).

2. Utilizes a "you" attitude by analyzing what the students want and how he can fill the bill.

3. Gives the necessary details and ends by confirming the time and place.

Forget It

The letter that says "no" or "forget it" to a special request is like the letter acknowledging an incomplete order—negative in nature and more difficult to write. However, your employer will at some time or another be asked for a favor or contribution which he will have to refuse.

On a sheet of paper, write a reply to the following situation.

The *Hi-Lite* staff (school newspaper) is attempting to pay part of its publication costs by selling psychedelic paper flowers made by the students. The secretary of the staff has written a letter to your employer, who is the vice president of the Towers Department Store at the Tremont Plaza Shopping Center, requesting one of the store windows to display the flowers from April 1 to 14. Towers Department Store has a company policy that only store merchandise can be displayed in its windows. Your employer takes great pride in the schools in his community and in no way wants to reflect an unenthusiastic attitude. He lacks authority, however, to change company policy.

The effectiveness of your communication can be judged by your answers to such questions as:

1. Did you begin your letter with a stereotyped, obvious beginning such as "Your letter of March 4 has been referred to me for a reply"?

2. Did you transmit a negative refusal like "unfortunately, we are unable to grant your request," before you gave any reasons?

3. Did you hide behind company policy, saying "Due to company policy, we will be unable to allow you to display your flowers in our windows"?

4. Did you present your reasons at a time in the letter when it was unimportant to the reader because he was already dejected by the brusque refusal? For example, "Many requests are made for the use of our windows for display, and unfortunately all requests cannot be met. Therefore, to avoid any partiality, we must refuse all who ask."

5. Then, did you remind your reader of the disappointment by adding "We hope that you will understand our reasons for refusing our display windows for your psychedelic paper flowers"?

6. Did you end your letter with a trite "If we can be of any assistance in the future, please contact us"?

If you find that you included any of the preceding, it is understandable. It is sometimes difficult to be tactful and considerate. Sometimes when you use the word *unfortunate* and express a desire to be understood, you feel that you have been sincere and considerate. However, to actually communicate sincerity and consideration in a refusal letter, you must do more than just use these words and thoughts. Probably the best way to write a refusal to a favor requested is to use an inductive sequence of ideas, such as:

1. Begin these letters with a neutral or positive beginning, such as "The *Hi-Lite* staff should be commended for developing ingenious ideas to raise money to finance their outstanding school newspaper."

2. Develop the reasons for not granting the request before actually refusing, so that the refusal can be more easily accepted. For example, "Last year Towers Department Store received more than 100 requests for use of their display windows by charities, high schools, colleges, church groups, and civic orga-

nizations. Who was to have priority? And when would it be possible to display store merchandise to customers who depend on these displays for latest styles and fashions?"

3. Refuse in the most positive manner possible, such as "For this reason, the management of the Towers Department Store has decided that display windows will be used for store merchandise only, so that customers can always rely on Towers to display the latest in fashions."

4. Include an alternative, if possible. For example, "Because we enjoy reading your high-caliber school newspaper as much as the students do, may I suggest that you have your business manager call me at 938-6521 to discuss advertising space in your next issue. You can count on us to advertise only things of interest to students."

5. End on a pleasant note, such as "Best wishes for another good newspaper publishing year. Perhaps you may want me to talk to some of my business associates about advertising in the *Hi-Lite*."

12

Just Plain Being Nice

Just as every letter should be a selling letter, every letter should also be a just plain "being nice" letter. The major difference is one of emphasis. For example, if a letter's primary purpose is just to be nice or promote goodwill, we can categorize the letter as strictly a goodwill letter, with any other idea subordinate. However, if the main theme of the letter is something other than a just plain "being nice" message, with goodwill subordinate to this main theme, we would refer to it as other than a goodwill letter in the strict sense of the word. The "being nice" letter is completely reader-oriented, with practically no emphasis on the writer. Because it involves a very personal approach, composing such a letter calls for a wide range of flexibility. Goodwill letters are usually letters of sympathy, appreciation, congratulation, praise; or announcements, invitations, or appointments.

Special Thanks

One of the "being nice" letters you will most likely be asked to write is one to show appreciation for something special done for you, and is the "special thanks" letter. Regardless of whether your reader expects some expression of appreciation or not, you should never neglect being well-mannered or just plain nice.

Timing is of utmost importance in writing a "special thanks" communication. Promptness indicates sincere appreciation. However, some appreciation or "special thanks" letters can be written at certain times of the year, rather than immediately following the action. For example, special thanks to prompt-paying customers may be best sent right after the New Year.

Since we have previously discussed the writing of routine thank-you letters, let's see if you can adapt or transfer your learning to the writing of a "special thanks" letter. How would you write a letter to your employer showing appreciation for a letter of recommendation written on your behalf? The fact that you are applying for a clerical position with the Peace Corps is incidental.

Would you remember to:

1. Lead off with the main message and tell your reader exactly why you were expressing thanks to him.

2. Or would you choose to lead up to a "special thanks" message after arousing the reader's interest with an attention-getter followed by a coverage of the facts?

Either of these openings could be used to show appreciation, providing that you unify the rest of the message by relating everything to appreciation.

Also, you must remember to:

1. Discuss any pertinent facts or observations.

2. Follow up with another "special thanks" in the form of returning a favor in the future, telling others, or remembering the deed.

This follow-up of appreciation will bring your reader pleasantly back to the good feeling of being appreciated. Avoid such trite, stereotyped expressions as "Your service is greatly appreciated." Cold and pompous reaffirmations of appreciation are worthless.

The following letter makes use of the above-listed suggestions in thanking a businessman who has unselfishly given his time to serve on a high school office-education advisory council.

Thank you for serving on the office-education advisory council for the past two years.

Your commitment to the school and to the community was reflected in your enthusiastic attendance at every council meeting. The program benefited especially by your experience and recommendations regarding the purchasing of modern equipment and typewriters for classroom use.

You may be sure that a copy of the minutes of every subsequent meeting will be sent to you for your examination. If you wish to comment on any of the recommendations that the advisory council is making to the school board, please feel free to call me. Actually, John, please continue being an advisor in an informal way.

Hats Off

Congratulations or "hats off" letters show thoughtfulness and good manners and are also considered just plain "being nice" letters.

These letters should be written:

1. *Promptly* (preferably the same day that the news is received).

2. *Enthusiastically*, with sincere interest in the reader (perhaps the beginning should be exclamatory).

3. *Informally*, with a conversational style when reviewing why the reader is being congratulated, and also informally in salutation and closing (use first name in salutation and avoid *yours* in closing).

4. *Reader-centered* (avoid everything extraneous to a "hats off" message to ensure unity of the letter—after all, attention should be on the reader).

5. *Sincerely* (avoid using "good luck," which may indicate to the reader that luck accomplished the feat).

Consider the following example of a businessman who congratulates a friend who has just won an election:

So you won the election! Congratulations to the new councilman of Palm Beach! It's another milestone in your fantastic business and political career.

Best wishes for continued success in both!

Analyze the following letter and consider its strong points. Then consider its weak points.

Another milestone has been passed in your development of the best youth organization in the state of Minnesota.

It is unreasonable to expect that my appreciation for your excellent and untiring work can be expressed by the mere writing of words on a sheet of paper. Satisfaction and gratitude for your accomplishments can only be in terms of the contribution to the development of the fine youth involved in the vocational clubs in our state.

It is to this end I would express not only my own appreciation, but the thanks of all the youth whom you have inspired and provided with leadership during the Leadership Conference. May you have the same good luck next year!

Would you agree that its strong points are its enthusiastic tone and its reader-centered message? Does it also appear to be a bit too formal? Would a more conversational style have been more effective? Did you approve the use of "good luck"? Do you think that the reader could interpret it to mean that the writer felt he was more lucky than capable?

The following letters are better examples of congratulatory messages because they are less stuffy-sounding and more sincere.

Social Business Congratulation to an Associate's Son

Congratulations, Jerry! You've accomplished quite a feat. Your parents must be as proud as we are here at General Products about the honors you achieved at Harvard.

Best wishes to you for the scholarship you received to study at Cambridge next year. We're sure that you will make the best of this experience just as you have with your entire college career.

Congratulations to a Person You Have Not Met, but Whom You Respect

Please add my congratulations to the many you have received on being selected as the recipient of the 19___ Chamber of Commerce Service Award. You must feel great pride in receiving such a recognition.

Because of your sacrifice and unselfish consideration for other human beings, you have brought hope to a group of aged in our city.

My best wishes for happiness in your life.

Personal Congratulation

Mary, I enthusiastically endorse the judgment of the Mothers Club of Yorkshire in naming you "The Mother of the Year."

You have made many fine contributions to the Mothers Club and to other community service organizations. You have set an example in our community for motherhood, love, and unselfish service.

Bill and the girls must feel very proud of you. Please accept my very personal best wishes, Mary. No one was more deserving of such an award than you.

Congratulatory Letter for a Company Anniversary

Dear David,

Congratulations on your twentieth anniversary with the Baxter Company. John D. Rockefeller once said, "The ability to deal with people is as perishable as sugar or coffee, and I will pay more for that ability than for any other under the sun." He would have had to pay you many dollars, David.

Although your accomplishments are numerous, your greatest contribution to Baxter has been your unusual ability to communicate with those you work for, those you work with, and those you supervise. This ability makes you vital to the functioning of Baxter's. What I am trying to say, friend, is we couldn't get along without you.

Best wishes for many more anniversaries and further success with "people problems."

Congratulations on Retirement (tone depends on relationship and personality of the person retiring)

Dear Miss Lazzetti:

All of us have been wondering what it will be like without friendly, anxious-to-be-of-assistance, Emily Lazzetti to greet each of us as we go to our offices each morning. We also worry about what our customers will think about us without your friendly reception.

You have been told many times of the important role you have played at Edward's since you joined us some thirty years ago; however, please allow me to add my tribute to you.

Miss Lazzetti, accept my personal gratitude for helping us be what we are today. Also, permit me to extend my best wishes for many years of happiness with your friends and family. We shall be most disappointed unless you visit us often—after all, Edward's is your home.

Sad News

News such as that of the death of a business associate or the serious illness of the wife of a customer can be another occasion when you can show thoughtfulness and be just plain nice. If the sad news concerns business associates only, you may use company stationery to express sympathy, as this will express sympathy from the entire company.

Letters of sympathy should be written:

1. *Promptly* (preferably on the same day you receive the news).

2. *Simply* (refer to the event that has occurred; then follow with an expression of sympathy).

3. *Sincerely* (use a serious tone, a statement of goodwill, and an offer to be of assistance).

The following letters are examples of appropriate replies to "sad news" letters.

Death of a Business Associate

All of us here at General Electronics are grieved by the news of the death of your president, Harry Jonathan. Please accept our most sincere sympathy.

Mr. Jonathan was a true leader and served as an example to all of us in the community. His charitable work with the Boy Scouts of America will long be remembered.

Yes, indeed, the memory of Harry Jonathan will serve as an inspiration to the members of the community of Green Plains.

Serious Illness

Your co-workers at Daffin Corporation are sorry to learn of the serious nature of your wife's illness. Please accept the flowers we have sent as sincere wishes that she will make both a fast and complete recovery.

All of us mean it when we say "Get well."

Offering Help in a Emergency

The FFA in Chanhassen is deeply concerned for the families in Savage who have had to vacate their homes until the rising Minnesota River reaches its crest and waters begin to subside.

May we offer the services of our FFA boys to help in sandbagging or any other way possible in assisting these unfortunate families? Our high school principal will excuse their absences from school if their services are needed.

Would you agree that the following letter of sympathy, sent to Mary Jackson, the receptionist at your office, whose son was killed recently in a tragic car accident, is sufficient in a time of deep grief?

Dear Mary,

Please accept my sincere sympathy in the death of your young son, David.

Since few words are consoling at a time like this, let me briefly say that my thoughts are with you and your family in this time of grief.

Hear Ye—Hear Ye

Announcements that tell your friends about something that has happened or is going to happen are also just "being nice" letters. Such "hear ye—hear ye" messages may be brief; and sometimes a single sentence suffices, such as "The Advisory Council of the Minnesota Business and Office Association will meet at the Civic Center at 7:30 p.m. on Monday, January 26, to discuss community survey plans."

For a lengthy announcement, you may wish to follow a plan of including with the announcement a discussion of reasons, and ending with a suggested action. Remember that the actual announcement is the major purpose of the "hear ye—hear ye" message. The following announcement is an example of a newly appointed executive director's message to the group he plans to work with:

Thank you for the opportunity to act as the Executive Director for the Delaware Chapter of the Distributive Clubs of America. Before the year is over, I hope to meet every member individually. All of us have a common goal—preparing youth for the distributive occupations.

I am enthusiastic about this new position and eager to get the activities going for this year. With your help we can make this DCA's best year in Delaware.

As your Executive Director, I plan to give this job all my attention and efforts. However, it will be you and your ideas and suggestions that will be the indicators of our future success. Let's rally together for a successful year.

Notice the tone and clear announcement in the following "hear ye—hear ye" message.

You will be pleased to know that the new Oreck's Store at River Road Shopping Center is now open and ready to serve you. Come in any time this week and next and help us celebrate our Grand Opening. A beautiful red rose is waiting for all the ladies who take part in the celebration.

Twenty-two different departments with modern, up-to-date settings and friendly, efficient salesclerks are eager to fill your shopping needs.

Do you agree that the second example below is an improvement over the first announcement? The tone gives the reader encouragement.

First Example

We have just recently sold our business to the Payton Company of Minneapolis, Minnesota. The Payton Company of Minnesota will in the near future be serving you, and needless to say we have told them about our many customers who have been so good to us in the past and they are excited.

We thank you for the many years that you have patronized Diamond, Inc., and we regret that we will no longer be serving you. Thanks for everything and also for the interest you have shown us in the past.

Some of you have been customers for many, many years and we appreciate very much your confidence. Yes, indeed, it is sad to leave a roster of 25,000 charge customers and many other cash customers.

Second Example

Thank you for being such a good customer for the many years that you visited Diamond, Inc.

Because we felt that to continue and to improve the goods and services to our valued customers would necessitate an investment beyond our means, we recently sold our interests in Diamond, Inc., to the Payton Company of Minneapolis, Minnesota.

Payton's is a fifty-year-old department store operation that enjoys the distinction, along with Swiggans and Oreck's, of successful, progressive retail selling.

It is with mixed emotions that we say goodbye to our roster of 25,000 charge customers and many other cash customers; however, it is with pride that we say we're leaving you in good hands.

In a Nutshell

Just plain "being nice" letters have a major purpose—just being nice. Remember, they should "turn on" your reader because you have shown thoughtfulness. Attention should be on the reader and little on the writer. Timing and sincerity are of utmost importance and will be determining factors in the success you have in being nice.

13

Sock It to 'Em

Every letter attempts to persuade a reader to accept its message. It is easy to see why many say "Every letter is a sales letter." In this chapter, however, sales letters or "sock it to 'em" letters will refer to the direct-mail type of selling of both products and services.

When you decide to use a direct-mail method of advertising and selling, you do so on the basis of a detailed study of costs and predictions of actual orders. Only if it would produce a profit margin large enough to cover the expenses involved in conducting this type of sales campaign would such an advertising and selling effort be adopted.

This process is costly and time-consuming and requires much thought. Once the decision is made, the process of turning out a sales-letter package is no less complex. Much preplanning, planning, and follow-up is involved. Research is necessary for complete understanding of both product and potential market. Then a time-consuming match between product and customer must take place. This is followed by an effort to present a vivid, positive sales message that will arouse interest, create intense desire, and persuade the reader to follow through by placing an order. Finally, the letter must be checked for completeness, conciseness, unity, readability, and persuasiveness. This final check will also include a critique of the typing and mechanics of the total sales-letter package.

Actually, few of you will have to do much of this type of writing. However, these letters can be of value to you. The "sock it to 'em" letter provides a challenge—you *have* to be persuasive in writing sales appeals letters—that will make other letter writing easier, especially letters of special request.

Another second reason for developing sales-letter-writing ability is the invaluable advantage of being able to appraise and evaluate the attempts of others, not to mention the practical personal applications that can be made.

Sock It to 'Em—How?

Just how you will "sock it to 'em" will involve careful preplanning and planning. You already have become acquainted with the requirements of a good request letter, such as a clear, definite request, motivating power to get favorable action to that request, and ease of response to the request. These basic elements are also the basic elements of the "sock it to 'em" letter. Everything else, such as devices to get interest and to create a desire for the product, is used to enhance these basic elements.

Get the Facts

In the "sock it to 'em" letter, getting the facts will mean that you must become fully aware of *what* and *to whom* you are trying to sell if you are to have any success in marketing your product or service.

What you are trying to sell must be conveyed to the reader in descriptive terms, such as the size, shape, color, and other physical qualities. It stands to reason that the more you know about what you are trying to sell, the easier it will be for you to direct your sales appeals. The description you give your reader will allow him to form a mental picture of your product or service. Yes, the description is very important; however, the functional use will be even more important. One should supplement the other.

Where will you go to find *what* you are trying to sell?

1. The product itself—physical characteristics, unique features, durability.
2. The materials that go into the product—variety used, source of supply.
3. The manner in which it is produced—kinds of equipment used, skills required, patents, sanitary measures.

Where will you go to find *who* will buy your product or service? Most often you will attempt to buy or rent lists comprised of prospective customers with common interests, like college graduates, high school graduates, magazine subscribers, teachers, and so on. Once you have selected the mailing list, you will need to know the following things about your prospective customer:

1. Is he a buyer or a jobber (one who sells to others)?
2. What is his background?
3. What are his needs?
4. What are his likes and dislikes?

Although in direct-mail advertising or selling the same letter is sent to all the prospective customers on the mailing list, every letter has to sound as though it were written especially for each reader. For this reason, research on the prospective customer is of great importance.

Have a Plan

Once you get the facts, your next step is to work out a plan—
a plan that will help you to include all that is necessary for developing a powerful, polished sales message. Remember, this
plan should include all of the requirements of a good request
letter and all the specifics that are necessary to the particular
situation. The following three-step plan is a suggestion that
could produce results for you:
1. Command attention and stimulate interest.
2. Describe and explain the product or service.
3. Motivate prompt, easy-to-take action.

Attention to Interest

The best way to prepare a strong sales message using this
three-step plan is to appeal to basic wants, because they are (1)
quickly aroused, (2) vigorous and strong, and (3) practically
universal. To illustrate the strength of basic wants and the
power that they have over people, here are two examples: "Remember the time your mouth was so dry you could 'spit cotton'?
You wanted water in the worst way" or "Remember the time
you were so hungry you could scarcely stand up? Just one piece
of bread, please, and never mind the butter."

Following is a list of the basic wants and the activators of
drives which make people go after what they want.

Basic Wants	*Appeals Derived from Them*
Food and drink	Enjoyment of appetizing and satis-fying food and drink

Comfort	Comfortable clothes, homes, and surroundings
Freedom from fear and danger	Elimination of fearful, painful, dangerous things
Superiority over others	Victory in every race—keeping up with the Joneses
Attraction of the opposite sex	Companionship, love, and affection of the opposite sex
Social approval	Acceptance by friends and associates
Welfare of loved ones	Provision for the welfare of loved ones
Longer life	Enjoyment of life—the possibility of living longer

There are other wants less basic. These are considered secondary and are learned or acquired. They develop as we grow older and become more experienced and conscious of our position in the community. For selling some products and services, appeals to these secondary wants can be very effective. Secondary wants are not, however, touched off as quickly as the basic wants.

Following is a list of secondary wants and examples of selling sentences that can touch them off:

Secondary Wants	*Examples*
Bargains	"Make $1 do the work of $4."
Information	"Comparison proves the new Finewell a great refrigerator to buy. Look at these features."
Cleanliness	"Before and after—see what a difference Tinsley Shampoo makes?"

Efficiency	"New Strumoil starts easier! Makes your engine cleaner, perform better, last longer."
Convenience	"A new instant coffee that tastes as good as your favorite ground coffee!"
Dependability, quality	"You can always count on a Wilson Job-rated Truck!"
Economy, profit	"Buy the economy size and save!" and "These tires give 33% more wear."
Curiosity	"Don't read this advertisement unless . . ."

The choice of your appeal is the result of the study of your prospective customers. And the appeal you choose will be the determinant in how you will develop the first step of your three-step plan for a successful "sock it to 'em" message.

It will be your job to arouse curiosity in your reader, so that he will be interested enough to read the beginning of your message. Any time you can make a reader ask "What in the world is this?" you have accomplished this objective, because the only way he can answer is to read on. The following attention-getters have been successfully used to attract readers enough to ask "Just what is this all about?"

1. Exciting, stirring, never-used-before statement in bold type or color.

2. A headline in bold type or color.

3. An illustration, such as a cartoon or clever drawing.

4. A gadget, such as a shiny new penny or a check.

It is wise to remember that whatever you use as your attention-getter, it should be positive, in good taste, and enticing. The only purpose of the attention-getting is to make the reader ask "What is this all about?" It will spark his interest; however, something more is needed if you expect the spark to catch fire. You must satisfy the interest you have aroused. There must be a bridge and a realistic connection to the main subject or you will offend your reader's intelligence. For example:

Have you noticed the beautiful stone drywall decorated with flowering shrubs and geraniums in front of your neighbor's home down the street? Whether you know your neighbor or not, you may want to take a look to see how sturdy the wall is, as well as how the decorative and colorful setting complements his two-story house.

Your home can have the same flair of natural charm in a distinctive setting that will complement your home for less than $200.

Avoid the following costly attention-getters, which have no relation to the subject of your letter:

1. Completely unrelated opening—"Beware Vicious Dog! We don't know if you have a dog or not, but we are willing to deliver to your door 26 baby spruce pine trees for an exceptionally low cost of $150."

2. Negative statements—"Are you ready to blow your brains out every day because you are plagued by door-to-door salesmen? Assuming that you are, we hope you will appreciate our selling of the Handi-Pak hairbrushes by mail."

3. Remarks insulting to a person's intelligence—"Have you heard that the early bird catches the worm?"

4. Lecture-sermon type of opening—"As a taxpayer, you should be vitally concerned with the expenditures of your city officials."

5. Kidding kind of opening—"Now you don't want to see me out of a job, do you? Well, if I can't sell you a new Speedy Vacuum, I may be out of a job."

You will find that the most effective attention-getters are those that allow the reader to picture himself pleasantly using the product or service—in other words, those that feature laborsaving, timesaving, moneysaving or other such advantages.

The following three attention-getting and interest-stimulating devices have been used in "sock it to 'em" letters. Following each is an analysis of its strong and weak points. Do you agree?

1. For three days beginning July 6 we offer our regular customers first choice in our annual advance clearance sale of boys' spring and summer clothing.

Strong Points	Weak Points
Factual	Not exciting or stirring
Complete	

2. You will probably spend the summer in Hawaii. Your plans are probably made, or maybe you've been just thinking about the trip and haven't attended to the details. If the latter is true, then allow me to invite you to call at this office and consult our travel experts.

Strong Points	Weak Points
Opening sentence is attention-getting and has sparked the reader's interest.	"Bridge" from the opening sentence to the product is unrelated.

3. It might interest you to figure this out: How much is it costing you for the maintenance of your present car?

Strong Points	Weak Points
The question for the opener entices the reader to read on.	Introductory clause is irrelevant and not necessary.

Description and Explanation

The second step in delivering an effective sales message is to describe and explain the product or service. You will, of course, have to cover its physical characteristics. If your reader is to understand the value of your product or service, he must have a vivid mental picture in his mind about it. He will not be able to appreciate your explanatory message that follows the description unless you have successfully conveyed this picture. Remember, it will be this description and the explanatory message that will be the significant factors in stimulating the reader to purchase the product. The description will be the introduction necessary to transpose the product or service into specific values to the reader. It will have to promise satisfaction of the reader's needs. Yes, it will carry the same reader-centered message as all request letters.

Do not try to bluff your reader. Just as the hard sell of the insincere salesman is recognized, the hard sell of the insincere message will be easily detected. Your product or service has to live up to your promises, through actual proof. A deliberate effort on your part to substantiate your claims—with actual evidence—will register positively with your reader. Many real-proof devices have been used successfully, such as:

1. Laboratory tests
2. Testimonials
3. Endorsements
4. Free samples
5. Trial periods
6. Money-back guarantees

The following lead attention-getters could be followed by the accompanying tie-in ideas:

1. "What shall I serve for the party?" (Lead selling cola)
"To many teens, the answer is automatically Wonder-Cola."

2. "Nothing smells so sweet down here in the pine woods as a fire started with quick-lighting Pitch Pine Kindling." (Lead selling kindling)

"Yes, your fire-starting problems are eliminated by merely striking a match to Pitch Pine Kindling."

3. "You don't need to be bald any longer." (Lead selling Easy-Care toupees)

"Easy-Care toupees will give you a healthy head of hair for that youthful look."

4. "Don't swelter this summer." (Lead selling Select-Air refrigeration units)

"Enjoy the cool, relaxed, comfortable hours of Select-Air refrigeration units."

5. "Cut strokes off your score with Tommy Jones nonslip golf shoes." (Lead selling Tommy Jones nonslip golf shoes)

"These shoes will give you the footing you need for a good golf stance."

Motivation to Action

The third step in the plan of an effective sales message is to motivate prompt, easy-to-take action. You must give a reason for your reader to act at once, because the highest pitch of interest is when the letter is still in his hands. You will probably have to induce him to take prompt action with industry prices, free trial periods, and free samples. All of these things will be ineffective, however, unless they are offered for a limited time only. This is the only way you will speed up your reader.

Motivating him to prompt action should also be accompanied by a helpful effort on your part. Payment plans and the opportunity to have delayed billing are examples of such helpful measures. Addressed, stamped envelopes are effective as well as convenient order forms. The easier you make it for the reader to answer, the more likely he will be to do so. If you expect a reader to answer by telephone, make sure the telephone number is obvious and that extension numbers are given for departments. If a personal visit is necessary, it is important that location be described and that store hours, parking facilities, and public transportation be indicated.

"Sock It to 'Em" Letter and Envelope Format

If you decide to use the sales letter in the direct-mail concept of selling, you must do just that—produce a sales letter. Your reader will expect a letter and not just a flyer, a leaflet, or some other type of brochure. If he opens the letter and finds a leaflet, he may think "Oh, just another advertisement" and flip it into the basket. Obviously, you won't be selling anything if he doesn't at least read the message. Therefore, one of the most challenging jobs you will have is to make the sales letter as individualized as possible, even though it is usually a form letter that will be sent to a common-interest mailing list of prospective customers. Usually it is impractical to use an inside address; therefore, you should attempt to attract attention and follow with a general salutation to the group, such as "Dear Student" or "Dear Homemaker." Also, using the exact date will probably be unwise, but since a date should be included, you could use "March, 1971," for example.

The sales letter permits you to use something besides words to maintain your reader's interest. Such things as layout, color, variety of type size, and gadgets can be used to attract attention and maintain interest. The other parts of the letter are basically the same as they would be for other types of business communications. Such things as the complimentary closing, company name, signature, and reference initials are all retained to keep the authentic look of a personalized communication.

Now you may realize how complex writing a sales letter can be. You must devote attention to the three-step plan, as well as coordinate the format so that it is unified and presents a total sales package.

Another important detail in developing the "sock it to 'em" letter is the envelope. As already stated, the amount of money and time spent in direct-mail selling will be futile unless the prospect reads the message. Your strategy should start, therefore, with the envelope itself. You may want to consider the following ideas that have been used to entice the prospective customer to open a letter and read it:

1. Make your correspondence resemble first-class mail (it will probably be third-class mail) by using precanceled stamps, imitation stamps, or metered mail.

2. Avoid using a return address, so that your customer will be curious enough to open the letter.

3. Use a tan-colored window envelope with the prospect's name showing, to give the impression that the enclosed material could be a bill, a bank statement, or a check.

4. Address the envelope in longhand to reduce the suggestion of mass mailings.

In general, however, mass mailings are difficult to camouflage, and some of the prospective customers will probably recognize them in spite of the above suggestions. To avoid being phony in these cases, it may be wise to be frank about the mailings and use an attention-getting device on the envelope, such as "Invitation enclosed" or "Free gift inside."

Three examples of sales-appeal letters that have been profitable to their companies are shown on pages 107 to 109. Notice the "sock it to 'em" effect.

"The Case of
the Missing Steak" . . . or . . . "It's Not As Rare
                                As You Think!!!"

Millions have laughed at the antics of "Freddie, the Freeloader" on television. Funny? Sure, because we all realize he is only a "make-believe" character. But his real-life counterpart is something else again! Especially the one who prefers to eat most of his meals "on the house" at his favorite restaurants.

Still funny? Not particularly, if *your* "house" is on his list! Chances are, if it *is* you aren't even aware of it! That's because the freeloader likes to *work*—and eat—with as little publicity as possible. He thrives on secrecy, and he has a good system going for him—which is more than many unsuspecting "hosts" can say!

Essentially, his system is very simple. Granted, he must spend a little time spotting establishments with a poor guest-check system and poor control over food and beverage requisitions. But from there on, it's all gravy—*with* meat and potatoes!

Add a dash of flattery, topped off with promises of a lavish tip, and an adept freeloader has the waitress in his hip pocket. You, of course, pocket the loss!

We have prepared a 12-page booklet which shows you how certain systems practically invite freeloader problems. It also includes a frank analysis of other risks and profit losses you take with a poor guest-check system.

To get your free copy of this vital information, just fill in the postage-free return card and drop it in the mail, today! Your booklet will be on its way by return mail. No obligation, of course.

Sincerely,

T. H. Flint, Manager
Supply Sales Division

N C R
The National Cash Register Company
Dayton, Ohio   45409

FUND FOR THE IMPROVEMENT
OF THE ENVIRONMENT

Dear Friend:

In past years we have promoted the need to free our environment from litter by distributing litter bags without charge. We appreciated your using them. It has been a tremendous help in reminding our community that the Fund for the Improvement of the Environment is devoted to making America a cleaner place in which to live.

Now we must reevaluate our total budget, because there is such a public demand for us to expand our community services. For this reason, we must discontinue the FIE tradition of distributing litter bags without charge.

Will you help us continue this worthwhile service by buying your litter bags and distributing them to your customers? You can buy them for as little as $4.70 per hundred.

Check the number you will need on the enclosed stamped business reply card today and return it to us. Your support will help FIE "Make America Beautiful."

Sincerely yours,

Mrs. Janet Smithe
Communications Director

SOMETHING JUST FOR YOU

Dear Teacher:

In a few days I'm going to send you 3 of the most exciting neck scarves for a week's FREE trial!

I mean it when I say, "You've never seen anything like them before . . . because there has never been another fabric like "Smasho"!

"Smasho" is a 50-50 blend of polyester and percale cotton. It is soft, yet strong, easy to tie, graceful, and flowing.

What's more, "Smasho" polyester cotton blend is washable and *needs no ironing.* Just throw the scarves into your washing machine. They drip or tumble dry ready to wear—smooth, soft, and wrinkle-free!

And these "Smasho" neck scarves *stay beautiful* all day—always looking fresh and alive! You'll never have that rumpled, wrinkled, drooped look with these easy-to-care-for accessories!

Their fantastic low price is unbelievable! Not $20, not $10, not even $6. But only $1.95 each! Unbelievable—but true.

Tell me your favorite colors on the handy enclosed card and mail it back to me today. I'll rush 3 exciting "Smasho" scarves to you for a *Week's Free Trial!*

You'll be glad you did!

Sincerely yours,

Mary Bradwahl
Fashion Director

Illustration 1 is an example of a direct-mail sales attempt using a gadget, as well as a play on words. Since steak is an attractive food to most people, such a vivid picture of one arouses interest. The play on words through "The Case of the Missing Steak" stimulates the reader's curiosity to search for completion of the statement by lifting up the steak (the steak was a "flap" attached to the top of the original letter). The use of the gadget in a sales letter is almost certain to take care of the problem of attracting attention. The gadget should complement, not dominate, the sales message.

Illustration 2 is a fund-raising letter which offers the reader an opportunity to support a cause. It differs from the sales letter in that it does not promise the prospect a product or a service. The abstract characteristic of such appeals limits you with regard to interest-creating gimmicks, explanation and proof, and urging to prompt action. The flashy beginning of the previously illustrated gadget letter would be in poor taste here. This opening should be more dignified. In a fund-raising letter you should identify the problem, tell your reader what has been done and what is being done to solve it, and attempt to involve him immediately. Your attempt should be to instill in your reader a feeling of wanting to "get on the bandwagon" and make a contribution.

Illustration 3 used different type styles and color to sell its message. The mailing list was women school teachers, and the appeal being made is one of savings and economy. The attempted proof of claims was made by enclosing swatches of material so that the reader could actually feel the fabric to check its "silky-smooth, wrinkle-free" qualities.

Tired of reading about how to write a "sock it to 'em" letter? Eager to write one? Try it anyway!

Assume you are a temporary summer helper at the Breezy Cape Lodge on Willow Lake outside Brainerd, Minnesota. Your boss is the sales and promotion manager. He just received a list of fishermen residing in the Minnesota area from the editor of the magazine *Outdoor Sportsman*. These prospects are prominent professional businessmen. It is now April 20, and he wants you to try your newly acquired sales-letter-writing skill by writing a letter urging these fishermen to spend their vacations at your lodge.

Since your resort is so popular, for the past two years you have had waiting lists; therefore, reservations should be made by May 10.

Some of the facts you might include in your letter are:

1. You have excellent bass and northern pike fishing.

2. You operate a charter plane service from Minneapolis to Willow Lake.

3. You require a $25 deposit for every reservation.

4. You have other facilities, such as boats, cabins, beaches, a nine-hole golf course, and a night club with dancing.

Perhaps your "sock it to 'em" letter should put particular emphasis on emotional appeals and descriptions. Obviously the pleasure, satisfaction, relaxation, and joy that a vacationer at your lodge can enjoy will be appealing to the busy businessman of today.

On a sheet of paper, write your sales-appeal letter. Remember, a total sales package will really "sock it to 'em."

Well, how many reservations do you think you'll get? Analyze your answers to the following questions and then make your predictions?

1. Did you attract attention and command interest in your opening message through words and eye appeal (color, layout, and so on)?

2. Did you attempt to study the product and your prospective customers so that you could match your lodge facilities with their vacation needs?

3. Did you use good grammar, correct spelling, logical paragraph development, and so on, so as to ensure accuracy in expressing your message in your reader's language?

4. Was your sales talk concerning the lodge honest and believable, possessing the ingredient of *proof* of your claims?

5. Did you lead logically, using emotional appeals, to your central theme—"vacationing at the Breezy Cape Lodge"?

6. Did you include a *specific* request (preferably a positive statement or command) with a final date for registering for lodge accommodations?

7. Did you make it easy for your customers to reply to your request for early reservations?

8. Did you include a descriptive brochure illustrating the lodge facilities, and did you remember to mention it in your letter? Were the facts in the brochure and the letter consistent?

If, in your final analysis, you can positively answer the preceding questions, you will undoubtedly "sock it to 'em" by getting more than your quota of lodge reservations!

The following letter brought in a "whopper" of a response:

How would you like to come home from a family fishing and vacation trip just once and be able to truthfully say "I got my limit every day"? To get your limit of bass and northern pike on Willow Lake is not extraordinary. Yes, bass and northern pike seem to thrive in this clear, spring-fed, deep lake nestled in the beautiful northern woods of everygreens two miles east of Brainerd, Minnesota.

"Vacationing at Breezy Cape Lodge," the article featured in the March *Outdoor Sportsman,* described in detail Breezy Cape Lodge on Willow Lake. Beautiful illustrations of fish-story-size catches and facilities depict what is awaiting you on your vacation this year.

Why not make a $25 deposit now to ensure your reservation and your free charter plane service from Minneapolis to Willow Lake? You will be assured an opportunity to do some serious fishing while your wife and family enjoy the modern heated cabins, white sand beaches, the great little three-par, nine-hole golf course, and the Olympic-size swimming pool, as well as the many other recreational facilities described in the enclosed color brochure.

14

Somebody Goofed

Sooner or later, in business as well as in everyday life, somebody will "goof." No matter how hard you try, no matter how carefully you design, produce, inspect, and package a product, something unexpected may occur. It is human to make errors. When these errors occur, you can usually count on the fact that a claim will be made against you requiring action on your part.

In the American enterprise system, "The customer is always right." And whether literally true or not, it should be true in theory. Every businessman should deal with customers in a manner that reflects that theory, because a businessman's success depends upon the customer's continued satisfaction with the goods and services that he receives. And your success depends on how well your letters can straighten out mistakes to your readers' satisfaction.

If you have goofed, you may be required to take large dosages of rudeness, unkindness, and outright temper flares. If you can control yourself in such cases and keep a calm appearance, you will have the best chance to get the customer to accept a fair settlement.

No matter who goofed, it is always improper to write an irritable, undiplomatic letter. No one has the right to abuse another person—not even if the other person is completely in the wrong. It will never be your turn to "get even." Businesses know that good public relations are the key to success. Millions of dollars are spent each year to relay this message to the public. It has taken several decades for good public relations to eliminate the "public be damned" image that was attributed to the industrialists of the 1900s. It would be ridiculous to jeopardize a good public image because of a hot temper. Also, it solves nothing to "fly off the handle."

I've Got a Problem

Let's say that you ordered a blue wool blanket from a mail-order firm. The blanket has just arrived, and you discover that the company has sent you a lime green blanket, not a blue one. You have a problem. You wish to have a blue blanket, as the color perfectly matches your room. You must write to the mail-order house and ask them to exchange the green blanket for a blue one.

Letters that make a claim or say "I've got a problem" must possess the essential qualities of diplomacy, exactness, positiveness, and a sense of fair play. Obviously, the manner of expression should never antagonize the reader. There is no need to get mad! Just as wars have never ensured peace, a loud mouth has never ensured the winning of an argument or the undoing of a wrong.

If you feel that you've got a problem because somebody goofed, it will be your responsibility to be exact and to describe the event completely by referring to date, time, place, order number, and other pertinent information. This is no time to be evasive. Also, remember no matter how negative or unpleasant the situation is, you must control your emotions, placing as little emphasis as possible on the negative aspects of the situation.

Lastly, you must make a reasonable claim; and in all fairness, you should give credit where credit is due. In other words, recognize the good points as well as the bad points.

"If you like our service, tell others; if you don't, tell us." Most businessmen, as this slogan shows, want to do right by you; and when they inadvertently do something wrong, they want to be notified so they can straighten things out. As a rule, they will meet you more than halfway. They know that happy customers come back again.

If you have a routine claim or "somebody goofed" message, the tone of your letter should reflect that you sincerely believe that the businessman wants to be told what has happened and will be eager to remedy the situation fairly.

Letter Format

Your first step in preparing the format for the "I've got a problem" letter is to recognize that the letter is basically a *request letter*. Therefore, it should comply with the letter format for request letters, such as stating a definite request, motivating the reader to reply to your request, and being as helpful as possible in allowing the reader to meet your request. However, other elements will have to be included in the "I've got a problem" letter.

Before making the actual request, it would probably be to your advantage to describe the situation and to explain how it has affected you. In other words, you will probably have to lay the groundwork before presenting your claim. In both the routine and the unusual claim letters, this groundwork is a necessity.

Routine claims are less serious in that they have a clear-cut course of action to follow. For example, nobody gets too excited about exchanging a lime green blanket for a blue one. In the more serious, out-of-the-ordinary "I've got a problem" letters, there will be less chance of an automatic settlement. Therefore, your special attention should be given to the motivation element —which brings us to the second step in preparing your letter format.

Definite appeals will have to be made, such as appeals to pride, honesty, fair play, and sometimes even fear. Naturally, an appeal to pride is less serious than appeals to honesty or fair play. Of course, the strongest would be an appeal to fear, and this appeal should be a last resort. One of the worst things you could do when resorting to fear would be to threaten in the opening sentence of the letter. This appeal should always follow an explanation and be toward the end of the letter. In all appeals you should remind the reader that his public image is at stake; and that to maintain his image, he should make a prompt adjustment.

The final step is to specifically state what adjustment you expect. Sometimes it will be to your advantage to explain when you expect such action to take place. However, act cautiously. Remember, you are to assume that you have a legitimate claim and that your reader will act promptly. This positive philosophy has been responsible for many automatic adjustments. Therefore, only demand settlement by a specific time if it will be helpful to the reader—unless you are using the appeal to fear, when a time limit is absolutely necessary.

A little over ten months ago, a young executive purchased an EXACTO desk clock and radio. After two weeks the clock stopped running every six hours or so. Since there was no local service for EXACTO timepieces in his city, he sent the clock back to EXACTO, Inc. After three months and two letters on his part, he got it back. But within two days, it was back to its old tricks—stopping every six hours or so. Of course, he is darn mad and emphatically writes a letter to EXACTO, Inc., asking them for permission to return the clock to the factory again. By the way, this time he wants results—not in three months but more like three days! He does have a problem! Assume you are the irate young executive and jot down a letter telling EX-ACTO about your problem.

1. Did you remember to describe the situation thoroughly and explain your position of having paid for a desk clock and radio ten months ago and still not having had the opportunity to enjoy it?

2. Did you motivate your reader by sounding an appeal to fair play?

3. Did you remember to alert your reader to the involvement of his image?

4. Did you also alert him to the fact that his image could be restored by either repairing the desk clock and radio or replacing it?

5. Did you specifically inform your reader as to what action you wanted?

6. Did you remember to keep your emotions intact, yet let your reader know you meant business?

7. Did your tone reflect a positive attitude, in that you believed that your reader was eager to remedy the situation and maintain your goodwill?

Now, compare your letter to the young executive's actual letter. Which one do you feel will get better results?

Over ten months ago I purchased an EXACTO desk clock and radio, Model No. LBX420, in a beautiful mahogany finish from Whitely's of Wayzata, Minnesota. For two weeks I enjoyed its beauty, sound, and precision; however, after two weeks it stopped running every five or six hours, so I mailed it back to your factory.

You can imagine how much I missed the desk clock and radio once I had enjoyed it, so naturally I became anxious when I had to wait three months to get it back.

Yes, indeed, it was a welcome sight last Monday when I received my repaired EXACTO. After two short days, and just as we were becoming reacquainted, it was up to its old trick—stopping every five or six hours.

Will you please allow me to return the clock for repair, or will you please replace it?

Next Tuesday, January 10, marks our 25th anniversary, and we are planning an open house. I would love to have my EXACTO desk clock and radio on my desk when my friends visit my office.

Sometimes Yes, Sometimes No

You may also be in the position of trying to straighten out things through a letter. The requests made in claim letters will sometimes allow you to say "yes" and force you at other times to say "no." Your job will be more difficult if you must refuse the claim or if the writer was most antagonistic and belligerent. In any case, you must keep your cool; you must use fact and finesse in dealing with the claim, and make sure that you do the following:

1. Answer promptly—don't antagonize the claimant further by delaying.

2. Make sure that your letter possesses all the qualities of the just plain "being nice" letter.

3. Never insinuate, when discussing the situation, that the person making the claim is an agitator or a troublemaker. Avoid negative terms like *your complaint* when you could say *your letter,* or *your unfortunate experience of April 10* when you could say *the April 10 incident.*

4. Give reasonable explanations. In the "sometimes yes" letter include only what is absolutely necessary in the explanation; however, in the "sometimes no" letter, be sure to explain before you turn him down.

The most challenging thing you will have to do is to convince the reader—right or wrong—that you maintain the philosophy that the customer is always right. His rudeness does not merit your rudeness. You should welcome this opportunity to give personal attention. In its own right, the adjustment letter is also a goodwill letter. It may also be an opportunity to rebuild or strengthen your image. Whether you must answer "yes" or "no" may not be your decision, but it will be up to you to know how to say it. Your goal should be: a friendship renewed.

Sometimes Yes

The easiest type of adjustment letter you will write is the one that allows you to say "yes" to a customer's claim. However, certain precautions should be taken:

1. Don't be too specific about the problem at hand.

2. Use nonoffending, neutral words in place of negative, offensive language.

3. Don't argue about who is at fault. If it is you, admit it and apologize; if it isn't, just forget it. Say "yes" and end it.

Letter format for the routine "sometimes yes" letter should include an opening that tells your reader that you are thinking alike. In a more serious situation where the person making the claim is hostile and angry, your opening should attempt to smooth things out before granting the request: "Thank you for informing us that your Order No. 26742, dated March 15, arrived two days after the Anniversary Sale. Of course, you may return the merchandise for full credit."

The next step in planning your "sometimes yes" letter is to grant the request. You will find that sometimes in the routine claim letter, granting the request is enough to tell your reader that you are thinking alike.

Thirdly, the "yes" letter may or may not demand an explanation. In routine letters where the request is granted, it is hardly necessary to explain.

The final step is to make an attempt to regain the confidence of the recipient. It is important that you sound convincing and sincere: "You will want to take advantage of the quantity savings discounts of White Sale items. These discounts are being offered early in July, with delivery ensured for the August White Sales." Don't make impossible promises, such as "We assure you that such a thing will *never* happen again."

Notice how the following sentences have been revised to lose their negative quality.

1. *Negative tone:* We are sorry that another error was made in your account. We apologize for the error.

More positive tone: Thank you for your letter of June 1 notifying us of your May balance.

2. *Negative tone:* Some time ago we were informed by you that a lamp you purchased from us was not in good condition because of damage in shipment.

More positive tone: Thank you for your letter of January 11 notifying us that the lamp in your Order No. 67420 was without a base.

3. *Negative tone:* We must apologize for our hasty refusal.

More positive tone: In our earnest desire to settle your claim promptly, we made a hasty decision regarding your request for a new shipment of Order No. 720.

4. *Negative tone?* As a matter of goodwill, we have decided not to charge you for the adjustments we have made on your radio.

More positive tone: You will be pleased to know that your EXACTO radio has been carefully repaired free of charge.

5. *Negative tone:* Don't worry, Mrs. Alfred, we'll exchange the clock.

More positive tone: If you will return the clock to us c.o.d. by parcel post, we will immediately replace it with a new one.

Sometimes No

There are times when it will be impossible for you to say "yes" to a request made by mail. It may be because the article returned is a sale item, the warranty on the article has expired, the article has performed as well as can reasonably be expected, or someone else such as the transportation company is at fault. Sometimes it will be necessary to say "no."

This will be bad news to the reader, but you don't need to write a negative letter. Instead, use tact and other skills of effective letter writing. It won't be necessary for you to refuse the writer outright. Imply rather than specifically state the refusal. In any case, the refusal, either expressed or implied, should follow a diplomatic explanation.

Thank you for taking advantage of the Daisy Sale on January 3–9. For the protection of all our customers, swimming suits must be fitted in our store and are not exchangeable. This store policy conforms to Health Regulation Law 231.

Before discussing the "sometimes no" letter any further, let's consider the following situation.

One of your candy customers, the Parker Drugstore, ordered 150 boxes of candy in assorted sizes for the Easter season. Slow payment on the part of the Parker Drugstore forced you to write two collection letters. Finally, they sent a check for 100 boxes sold and asked if they could return the other 50 boxes for a credit of $102. Because they have given you their business for the past five years, you are not eager to lose them as a customer. But candy is a perishable item, and should always be fresh and stored at normal room temperature. You cannot possibly do business the way they want you to. You would be encouraging customers to overorder, and you would find yourself in the position of having to accept hard, stale, dry candy. This type of service would be costly and unprofitable. Your boss has just breezed into your office and said: "That Frank Evans at Parker Drug must be losing his mind. Why, we would have to double our prices to cover losses if we did it his way. Write to him immediately and refuse the adjustment he requests."

Write a "sometimes no" letter, but don't forget that Frank Evans is a paying customer.

Well, how did you do? Not as easy as saying "Yes, Frank, you may return the 50 boxes of candy," was it? Evaluate your letter using the following criteria:

a. Was your overall philosophy diplomatic? In other words, did you turn him down but still make him feel that you did everything possible to help him out?

b. Did you attempt to clear yourself of any blame that Mr. Evans could place on you for refusing to accept the candy?

c. Were you as positive as possible in your attempt to explain your refusal to accept the candy before actually doing so?

d. Did you imply a refusal rather than express it explicitly, so as to make the refusal less painful to the customer?

e. Did you attempt to be helpful, such as suggesting a new sales promotion idea to move the 50 boxes of candy that were not sold at Easter?

f. Did you attempt a subtle technique in your implied refusal, such as moving smoothly but rapidly to a new subject? Once again, you might have used the sales promotion idea. This technique can communicate refusal without explicitly expressing it.

Notice how the following sentences have been revised to lessen their negative quality. Do you agree that the more positive tone of the revised sentences succeeds in "cushioning the blow" and makes the "no" easier to take?

a. *Negative tone:* There really doesn't seem to be any evidence that we are at fault regarding your claim; however, we will check into it.

More positive tone: Thank you for notifying us regarding your unfilled order of May 10. You will be pleased to know that a tracer was immediately put into effect, as the order was mailed to you on May 12.

b. *Negative tone:* It is the policy of our store not to allow the return of electric razors for sanitary reasons.

More positive tone: For your protection all electric razors are nonreturnable.

c. *Negative tone:* To avoid problems like the one you just had, you should study more carefully the directions we took so much trouble to prepare for you in the instruction manual.

More positive tone: You will find our instructional manual clear and easy to follow. To ensure completely safe operation of your Boro Rotary Lawn Mower, please read it carefully.

d. *Negative tone:* You realize that we certainly cannot take back merchandise that you have used, as is obvious by the condition of the returned trousers.

More positive tone: Customers have a right to brand-new merchandise when they buy at our store or any retail store. Because we work hard to please you and our other valued customers, we exchange only merchandise that has not been worn.

Somebody Did Goof

Obviously, somebody did goof if a customer takes time to write a complaint letter. These requests for adjustments and the answers to these requests are letters that should be viewed as opportunities to make direct contact with customers.

A claim letter or a letter making a complaint is by its very nature unpleasant. However, the letter you write making the claim does not have to sound unpleasant, especially if you steer clear of the following:

1. Reporting an incident when you are highly emotional.
2. Referring to the difficulty repeatedly.

3. Using threats as the rule rather than as the exception to the rule.

4. Giving insufficient information, so that the reader has difficulty interpreting the message.

5. Attempting to express "It's your fault, so what are you going to do about it?"

Of course, the letter that you write responding to a "somebody goofed" letter must also be a pleasant communication, no matter whether you are saying "yes" or "no." Attempting to do the following things should help you:

1. Make a decision as to what course of action you will take.

2. Write a letter that conveys this decision explicitly.

3. Begin your letter on an agreeable note, no matter what your decision is.

4. Be kind and diplomatic, no matter how unkind or undiplomatic the writer was when he made his claim.

5. Avoid an apology if there is no need for one.

6. Don't argue; it won't help.

7. Build goodwill by being as helpful as possible.

15

Short on Cash, Long on Character

The "buy now, pay later" philosophy seems to be in, to such an extent that we have all been referred to as the credit-card crowd. Yes, the "pay as you go" and "cash and carry" philosophies of yesterday are quite outmoded. Today we sell vacations on credit, and even burial plots.

There are two types of business credit—retail credit, which is available to you as a consumer; and trade or mecantile credit, which is available to a dealer from his supplier.

Before either retail or mercantile credit is issued, however, the customer must make formal application. The firm granting credit will obtain the customer's credit rating. It is common in mercantile credit to refer to a credit agency such as Dun & Bradstreet. For retail credit, a credit rating may be secured by asking the applicant for references and writing to them.

Retail Credit

The credit card is very popular in retail credit and serves as an identification at the time of purchase. Credit cards may include an expiration date so as to force the customer into a probationary period. The latest type of charge card is the bank credit card, such as BANK AMERICARD and MASTER CHARGE. Merchants who honor the cards can receive an immediate payment from the bank, which acts as the clearinghouse for credit charges and collections. This type of charge card is gaining in popularity because it allows the small merchant the advantages of offering credit. Probably the most attractive feature is the fact that check writing is held to a minimum.

There are several different arrangements that can be made for retail credit, depending upon company preference. The three most popular kinds of retail credit are:

1. The regular charge account, which issues the customer an identification plate. (Large charges must be verified.) Usually a statement is sent at the end of each month for this type of credit, and the amount is payable on receipt of the statement. Cycle billing is used for regular charge accounts so as to ensure a free flow of money into the firm. Billing is done according to alphabetic sequence of last names at designated dates. This type of charge account gives the customer the greatest credit freedom.

2. Revolving credit. This is the same as the regular charge account, with one basic difference. The entire bill does not have to be paid upon receipt of the statement, and a carrying charge is added to the balance. This charge may appear to be a disadvantage; however, the customer can enjoy the benefit of charging as much as he wishes and still make small payments.

3. The lay-away plan. With this plan the customer pays a small percentage down and asks the company to hold the item for him. The customer does not take possession of any merchandise until he has paid for it. He also has the privilege of making small periodic payments until he finally pays for it in full and picks up the item.

Mercantile Credit

Trade or mercantile credit is entirely different from retail credit. This type of credit is extended from supplier to manufacturer, from manufacturer to jobber, and from jobber to retailer. Usually a "line of credit" (a specified limit) is extended to the customer. Purchases are made during a one-month period, and monthly statements may or may not be sent out at the end of the period, depending upon the company's preference.

A customary feature of trade or mercantile credit is a cash discount (savings on regular price) granted to customers who pay within a specified number of days. Such credit terms as 2/10, n/30 are stated on the invoice, which means a 2 percent discount will be given for payment made within 10 days; the total (net) is due in 30 days.

Another popular type of mercantile credit is that of shipping goods on consignment. Under this arrangement, title to the goods remains with the seller. The buyer is required to send periodic reports and payments for the items sold. The supplier has to underwrite the whole operation, which could be a financial burden; however, such an arrangement may be necessary if he is in desperate need of retail outlets.

Have Faith—in Me!

The credit letter, which is in essence a plea to "have faith—in me," follows the same format as that of a special-request letter, whether this request is for retail credit or mercantile credit. Obviously, because selling is handled more and more on a face-to-face basis, written requests for credit or "have faith—in me" requests are also handled on a face-to-face basis. Therefore, requests made on forms along with personal interviews are most commonly used to initiate credit applications. In mercantile credit, where businesses are seeking "lines of credit" from distant suppliers, requests for credit are made in writing.

Even if such a letter is infrequently used, when it is, it is of such significance you should know how to write one. If credit is "tight" or difficult to secure, the ability to write a credit letter is even more important.

The writer of the following letter has been purchasing many goods and services from the Great-Line Company catalog during the past six months. He was pleased with their merchandise and service so he decides to write to them, sending all the available information he thinks would be necessary to establish a regular charge account. Obviously, it wasn't feasible for him to fly to Chicago from Minneapolis to make a face-to-face request!

The service that the Great-Line Company provides its mail-order customers is unbelievably efficient.

Since I have purchased more than $400 worth of merchandise from your catalog during the past six months, I feel qualified to make such a remark.

With Christmas only two months away, however, I have many more purchases to make and would like to avoid the c.o.d. inconvenience. Will you please consider my application for a 30-day regular charge account? I realize, of course, that I would be billed once a month and that payment is due ten days after receipt of my statement.

For the past five years I have been employed as a cashier for the Monica Investment Company and am not married. Both my checking and savings accounts are with the First Iron Bank of Alaska. I have regular charge accounts at Chesters and Davidsons, as well as a New Jersey BANK AMERICARD. If you grant my credit request by the first of next week, I will have a whole month of buying before the Christmas rush.

Let's see if his "have faith—in me" request for retail credit has all the elements necessary to effectively persuade the Great-Line Company credit department.

1. Did he make a direct request after a brief buffer-type statement that showed his reader the advantage of granting him credit? ("For the past six months I have ordered more than $400 worth of merchandise on a c.o.d. basis from the Great-Line Company. With Christmas only two months away, I have many purchases to make. Will you please consider my application for a 30-day regular charge account?")

2. Did he make a good transition from the opening buffer to persuasive evidence by striking with a strong argument? ("A regular charge account would allow me to buy more now—before the Christmas rush.")

3. Did he make the request and terms specific and convince the supplier that he intends to meet the terms?

4. Did he end his letter with a mild request for action, rather than the high-pressure "sell"? In other words, did he give his reader the prerogative of refusing his request?

A good philosophy to have when requesting credit is to sell your reader on the idea that mutual profits can evolve if he accepts your "have faith—in me" request.

Welcome—You're In

If after checking your applicant's credit references and other information you decide to grant him credit, you should be direct when you say "Welcome—you're in!" The reader will want to know immediately that his credit is granted, so why beat around the bush? As indicated in "welcome—you're in," the opening statement should include more than merely the good news. It should get the relationship off to a good start by making your reader aware of being "in" as far as your family of customers is concerned. Your opening statement should reflect the warmth and sincerity of your just "being nice" letters in its attempt to build goodwill.

The format of your "welcome—you're in" letter should be as follows:

1. Grant the credit request and welcome your new charge account customer enthusiastically. Even if you have had a hard time reaching a favorable decision, you should avoid any hint of a grudging tone, stiffness, or formality.

2. Describe the terms and other arrangements so that the reader clearly understands them. Describe the terms in a neutral tone rather than a scolding tone.

3. Close with a goodwill statement which mentions the advantages of the charge account, such as free parking, delivery service, and perhaps a forthcoming sale.

The letter that is written granting credit will follow the same format for both retail and mercantile trade credit. Notice the stiff and crisp tone of the first "welcome—you're in" letter that follows. Then notice how use of the format described above has made it easy to effectively rewrite the letter.

We are glad to grant you the credit that you recently asked for. We want you to understand clearly that your account will carry a limit of $500 and that bills sent on the 15th of each month are payable by the 30th of the following month.

Also, we hope you appreciate the privilege of credit with us.

Congratulations! Credit up to $500 has been granted to you as requested in your letter of June 1.

Your regular 30-day account will allow you to charge up to $500 a month. Your statement will be sent to you on the 15th of each month. It is payable within 45 days.

You will enjoy the convenience of buying now and paying later, the ease of telephone ordering, and the special savings for regular charge customers. Use your new charge account privileges at Great-Line's Daisy Sale coming up July 3.

Not Now—Maybe Later

Here's a tough one. How would you answer the following letter from Mrs. Thomas Keenan? Your mail-order house cannot extend credit to her no matter how honest she appears to be. Write your answer on a sheet of paper.

I think your catalog is better than ever, and I mean it! Your bargains have saved me money and your service has saved me time. I would like to apply for your regular charge account privileges.

I have many references as to my honesty. My husband is dead and I collect $198 a month in social security benefits. I take care of kids for my neighbors and do washing and ironing. Sometimes I earn up to $40 a month doing this extra work.

My kids are good kids and all five of them, from the seven-year-old to the one-year-old, are well behaved and helpful around our house.

I could use your help, so please consider my charge application.

Tough one to say "no" to? Sure it was. It's never easy to say "Not now—maybe later," especially when the request appears to be so honest and so necessary. You should have been very tactful when you refused this customer, and you should have followed the format used when declining or refusing any special request, such as:

1. Did you open your letter with a statement of appreciation for the writer's request, a buffer statement to set the stage for the refusal?

2. Did you make a good transition from the buffer, which showed appreciation, to your explanation of why you had to refuse? Did you do so before you actually refused?

3. Did you use a good "you" attitude in this transition?

4. Did you imply the refusal tactfully, or did you express it specifically? If you did express the refusal, were you clear and positive rather than negative?

5. Did you make concrete, helpful suggestions as to what action she could take now?

6. Did you remember to encourage continuation of cash sales business?

7. Did you close with the hope-for-the-future attitude? Did you attempt to keep your customer's goodwill?

If you made favorable answers to the question checklist, you probably lessened the blow of your refusal to this honest woman's request for credit. Also, you probably retained her as a cash-paying customer—a letter-writing skill to be envied.

The following letter to Mrs. Keenan has lessened the blow by its "hope-for-the-future" tone:

Thank you, Mrs. Keenan, for your kind remarks about our new catalog and for being a regular cash-purchase customer for more than ten years.

You have remained a cash customer of ours for so many years, we are sure, because of our low prices and quality merchandise. Savings to customers, however, are only possible when losses are low.

To protect ourselves from losses, thereby ensuring low prices and greater savings to our customers, we only grant credit to those who earn a minimum of $300 monthly. When your monthly income reaches the $300 minimum, we will enthusiastically grant you credit.

Until then, take advantage of the great savings for both cash and credit customers at our Krazy Day Sale beginning Saturday, June 10.

Remember, in "welcome—you're in" letters you are primarily concerned with complete, clear coverage of the credit terms so as to avoid future misunderstandings. In the "not now—maybe later" letters you are primarily concerned with explaining the refusal before actual refusal is made, so as to retain your applicant as a cash-paying customer.

16

Pay Up

Although a collection series involves a rather sophisticated letter-writing skill, at this point in your development it is extremely wise to "spread your wings" a bit and see for yourself what you really know about letter writing. If you can learn to successfully complete an effective collection series, you have reached a high level of letter-writing skill. Your ability to write positive letters, to reflect the "you" attitude, to motivate to action, and so on will be put to its most grueling test. In this chapter most emphasis will be placed on nonpersonal collection letters, since most collection letters are written by businesses.

Whenever credit is extended to any degree, collection or "pay up" letters are sure to follow. Not all promises to pay up are kept. Sometimes the customer forgets to pay, sometimes he puts off paying temporarily, sometimes he fails to pay because of a problem, and sometimes he doesn't pay because he just doesn't feel like it.

In many large companies, credit and collection departments are maintained to encourage customers to pay up. Obviously, profits are made through sales. Therefore, salespeople want to sign up as many customers as possible. The people who work in the credit and collection departments are somewhat less enthusiastic than the salespeople about signing up customers. They move more cautiously and tend to hold out for first-rate credit customers only. Since "pay up" letters are usually the responsibility of credit and collection departments, you can understand why they tend to be wary. The conflict between these two departments can be readily recognized. The credit and collection departments would like to have 100 percent restitution. The sales departments frown on forceful methods of collection, because their desire is to retain the customers' business.

"Pay Up" Letter Format

It makes good sense to design "pay up" letters that are dual-purposed in their attempt to collect debts and maintain goodwill—getting the money and keeping the customer. Even though you may feel that you have the right to seek what is yours and that the customer has violated his agreement, you still should maintain the profit-motivated philosophy that "the customer is always right." You should still cater to his goodwill. Therefore, you must hold anger and disgust in check. Probably the most important thing you can do in opening your letter is to encourage him to read it to the end.

Strictly speaking, collection suggests a physical act, and you will never actually have the power to collect money. Therefore, to put "pay up" letters in perspective, your challenge is to design and organize a series of letters that will *persuade* or *sell* the reader that it will be to his advantage to pay up promptly. Avoid scolding or sermon-type letters. They will only bore and antagonize him. You should attempt to develop a program or series of letters based on the trust you had in granting the credit in the first place. Your program should attempt to persuade him to develop better paying habits as well as to keep him as a customer.

Persuading customers to pay up is by its very nature negative and reflects on their personal integrity and honor. Therefore, writing "pay up" letters will require careful planning and organization on your part.

Once credit and collection departments recognize delinquent accounts, they attempt to make a systematic, yet flexible, plan for collection. Usually a series of contacts that get progressively more forceful is made. This continues until payment is made or the effort to get the customer to pay up is unsuccessful. Most companies proceed through four stages in their effort to persuade the customer to pay up.

First Stage

The first stage is usually the notification. It begins when the account first becomes delinquent and is continued until negative results are obvious. Some firms send out a second or third statement, which is usually a duplicate copy of the original. When it seems necessary, a printed notice or sticker which informally requests payment is often attached. This type of reminder is usually mild and quite impersonal.

Second Stage

The second stage is a letter sent in place of the impersonal reminder. This letter is usually very mild and attempts to promote goodwill.

Third Stage

The third stage, the discussion stage, is actually the meat of the collection series. It begins when you no longer believe that the customer *will pay*. He will have to be sold on the idea that he *should pay*. Sometimes a series of letters is sent during this stage, built around a variety of appeals designed to persuade the customer to pay up.

Fourth Stage

The fourth stage follows when all else has failed. Usually this is only one letter with a final chance for the customer to pay up before any last-resort action is taken, such as turning the delinquent account over to a collection agency or to an attorney.

Reminders

Notifying your customer of his delinquent account is the first step in the collection series. At this stage you still feel that the customer will pay; therefore, hopefully, the reminders will either extract payment or produce an explanation of why payment has not been made. Undoubtedly, these are impersonal appeals, with the first one possibly a duplicate of the original invoice. Then it is followed by a more intense effort, wherein the statement may have a rubber-stamped overdue reminder, such as:

PLEASE PAY   YOUR ACCOUNT IS
NOW—OVERDUE   PAST DUE

or a sticker with an overdue reminder attached to the invoice, such as:

PROTECT YOUR CREDIT   YOUR ACCOUNT IS
RATING—PAY NOW   ——DAYS OVERDUE

Remember, these reminders are used first because you feel that the customer will pay and that he will do so promptly.

The First "Pay Up" Notice or Letter

Naturally, all credit and collection departments hope that the reminders sent out with the "customer will pay" philosophy will be successful and that payment will be made promptly. How easy life would be! Unfortunately, it has been well established that some customers will not make restitution; therefore, it will be necessary to prod these customers some more.

Several means of communication can be used effectively. A face-to-face relationship would probably prove the most effective (if it would be feasible for you to visit him or if he could be encouraged to come in). Also, a telephone conversation would be personal and effective. Both of these means would be practical only if distance wasn't a factor. The telegram can also be used to spur the customer to pay up. It has the advantage of attracting attention and making the customer aware of the seriousness of the situation. Telegrams suggest urgency—sometimes effective in attempting to collect money.

But the "pay up" letter is the most common means of prodding the customer during the "customer will pay" stage of collection. This letter is sent when impersonal reminders have failed to produce payment. The letter is mildly worded, courteous, and helpful. It may or may not be a form letter. It may be preprinted or individually typed. Because of the upsurge in the use of the automatic typewriter, magnetic tape Selectric typewriter, and so on, the trend is toward individually typed letters rather than the form letter fill-in type. Examples of both follow:

INDIVIDUALLY TYPED FORM LETTER

Dear Mrs. Jones:

This is to remind you that your account, No. 6742, amounting to $564.42 is now three months past due.

If you have already mailed us your check, please disregard this notice. If not, use the enclosed, stamped envelope to send us your check for $564.42 today.

Sincerely yours,

FILL-IN FORM LETTER

Gentlemen:

This is to inform you that—is now three months past due on your account, No.—.

Please remember that your credit was granted with the understanding that payment would be made under terms of Net 30 days.

Please mail your check for—in the enclosed stamped, addressed envelope today!

Sincerely yours,

Then . . . "You Ought to Pay" Letters

Obviously, if you haven't heard from the customer after the reminders and the first "pay up" letter, you can reasonably conclude that the customer *will not* pay. It is then your responsibility to persuade him that he *ought to pay*. This stage is the *challenge* of your series. It will be your choice to write one or more letters designed to use various appeals to induce your reader to pay.

It will be necessary to plan this letter or letters to:

1. Arouse interest by doing something unexpected. Don't forget, he has received your reminders; therefore, even before he opens the envelope he will expect an "according to our records" or "Your account is now—months past due." Don't rehash what has already been ignored. Use a new approach. Open with a statement that will catch his interest as well as motivate a reply.

2. Motivate through carefully chosen appeals. Let such things as customer relationships, amount involved, and previous correspondence serve as your guide. Frequently used appeals are as follows:

Ego. Emotional appeal showing how his self-pride, ego, and reputation are at stake and that prompt payment can restore his *image*.

Sympathy. Emotional appeal telling the debtor that you need the money to keep going. This appeal is usually used when you and your debtor are good friends. It should be used with discretion, however, as it is sometimes interpreted as "Oh, oh. They're in financial difficulty."

Cooperation. Logical appeal inviting the customer to discuss his case with you. This logical appeal may be used to induce the customer to make partial payment, by showing him that you are open-minded and understanding and willing to work with him.

Economy. Logical appeal showing the debtor how economy results when prompt payment is made. Prompt payment means lower operating costs, and lower operating costs mean lower customer prices.

Fear. Emotional appeal telling the debtor of drastic action that must follow in the form of canceling the credit privilege, turning the account over to a collection agency, or repossessing the goods. This appeal can be used when all others have failed.

Although the different appeals have been listed separately, you may wish to use more than one in the "customer ought to pay" letter or letters.

3. Make it clear what you expect the reader to do. If you must have full payment, make it clear. If partial payment will be acceptable, make it clear also. Make sure that you restate the amount due and identify the account so the customer has no opportunity to misinterpret it. Since the account is long past due, immediate payment is expected.

4. Be helpful to your reader by making action easy through physical assistance, such as stamped, addressed envelopes or ad-

dressed envelopes without stamps. In either case, they are helpful and also serve as another reminder to pay up!

Finally—You Must Pay

The "you must pay" stage is the final stage in the collection
series. It usually consists of "a one-more chance" letter giving
the reader a final opportunity to pay before you take last-resort
action, such as turning the account over to an attorney or a
collection agency. Fortunately, most delinquent customers pay
or make arrangements to pay before this stage is reached; however, some "you must pay" letters have to be written.

Last-resort action is commonly turned over to a collection
agency for delinquent retail credit accounts and to larger credit
exchange houses for delinquent mercantile or trade accounts.
These agencies use rigorous collection methods, as well as the
exchange of delinquent-customer information, which could advertise the customer's bad record.

You should attempt to design this final "pay up" letter
forcefully—with collection talk from beginning to end. This letter should:

1. Begin with a direct statement of the action to be taken if
payment is not made *immediately*. You can precede the direct
statement with an explanation telling why it is being taken, like
"Your account No. 6246 for $1,244 is ten months past due; there-
fore, you leave us no choice but to turn this over to the collection agency for legal action."

2. Make a logical transition to an explanation of what such
last-resort action will mean to the reader. You should attempt to
convince him that he cannot afford *not* to pay, and point out the
negative implications.

3. Make a final pitch for payment. Set the deadline for payment or for making arrangement for payment and urge him to

meet the deadline, such as "It's in your hands now. Yes, only you can save your credit rating and prevent legal action."

4. Make one final plea for partial payment (if this is acceptable) or any other suggestion to help improve the debtor's position, such as "We'll hold off the collection agency until July 10."

To really put your letter-writing ability to test, try writing a collection series for the following delinquent account for the hospital where you are a volunteer worker.

You realize one of the big problems in operating a hospital is collecting from patients who have been discharged. Whereas a business firm can refuse credit to a delinquent customer, hospitals seldom refuse admission to a person who needs hospital care, even if that person has a delinquent account with the hospital. However, just as the business firm can use the last-resort services of a collection agency, hospitals can also use the services of the Medical Collection Agency. The resale appeal is possible for hospital collection letters just as it is for business firms, because the hospitals offer service on a nonprofit basis.

Your debtor in this case is Harvey Swartz. He owes $245.60 for the hospitalization of his wife, Andrea, who fell down her basement stairs and broke her elbow. Although the injuries were not too serious, she was in the hospital three days for observation, X rays, and bonesetting. Unfortunately, Mr. Swartz carries insurance only for the doctor's services.

It will be your choice as to how many letters you wish to include in the series. Begin the series with a form letter, which is described in the "customer will pay" stage. Also, write as many letters as you think this problem requires when you are making your appeal in the "customer ought to pay" stage; and, of course, one letter should be written in the last-resort-action "must pay" stage.

After writing two or three reminders like the ones illustrated in this chapter on pages 137–38, compare your "will pay," "ought to pay," and "must pay," letters with the following:

"Will Pay" Stage

This is our second letter reminding you, Mr. Swartz, that you still owe Hennepin Hospital $245.60.

When you made application for admission and asked for hospital care, we gave it immediately, explaining that payment was due in 30 days.

Your remittance of $245.60, mailed in the stamped, addressed envelope, must be returned today.

"Ought to Pay" Stage

Dear Mr. Swartz:

Won't you allow us to help you once again as we did when we admitted and cared for your wife, Andrea, for three days after her fall on June 17.

Just as we welcomed her into the hospital, we would welcome any explanation or comments from you now regarding your long-past-due account of $245.60. A few words from you may be to our mutual advantage. Perhaps we may once again help by arranging small monthly payments. All you need do is ask.

Enclosed is a stamped, addressed envelope for your convenience in sending us your check—or at least a note explaining your situation.

"Must Pay" Stage

Dear Mr. Swartz:

This letter is of utmost urgency and requires your undivided attention.

Monday, December 2, is the deadline. If a check from you for $245.60 for the hospitalization of your wife, Andrea, from June 1–3 for observation, X rays, and bonesetting is not in our hands, we must take legal action. This is necessary to ensure our ability to answer other patients' pleas for help as we did yours and your wife's last June. Our only recourse is to turn this unpaid account over to the Medical Collection Agency on that date.

You still have time to use the enclosed, stamped envelope and send us your check for $245.60 today so that it reaches us before December 2.

17

Here Comes the Judge

Mary Beth Ryan has submitted her resignation as Mr. Jonathan Davis' secretary, and for weeks he has been frantically reading application letters and résumés in search of a replacement. Mary Beth couldn't help but think "Thank goodness! He's finally found someone" when he rushed to her desk one day and said: "Mary Beth, if this girl is as good as this letter makes her sound, I'm going to let you get married next month. Just read it and judge for yourself. If you don't agree that this applicant looks mighty good, I'll give you a two-day vacation with pay."

(See Illustrations 1 and 2 on pages 144–46.)

If you were Mary Beth, how would you judge Pam Eckers' letter? Would you grant her an interview? Now remember, don't let that two-day vacation with pay influence your decision. Judge the applicant by her letter and her résumé.

Pam's approach to applying for this job is one of the most popular. She sent a résumé (summary of her overall qualifications) and a separate letter of application. Of course, the résumé has direct bearing on the letter and the letter has direct bearing on the résumé.

ILLUSTRATION 1

3421 Texas Avenue
St. Louis Park, MN 55426
March 4, 1971

Mr. L. B. Smith, Personnel Director
Office Services Unlimited
P.O. Box 7007
Jacksonville, FL 30236

Dear Mr. Smith:

Mrs. Rosemary Blackstone, my office coordinator, has informed me of a secretarial vacancy in your firm. Will you please consider me an enthusiastic applicant?

I will be graduated from St. Louis Park Senior High School, St. Louis Park, Minnesota 55426, on June 4, 1971, where I maintained a B average and an excellent attendance record. During my senior year, I was selected from among 100 applicants to be a member of the Office Education Cooperative Part-Time Training Program. This program allowed me to complete classwork each morning and to gain on-the-job experience with a professional office worker every afternoon. Needless to say, it became necessary for me to mature quickly, because of this dual role of student and worker.

As you will notice on my enclosed data sheet, I have actively participated in extracurricular activities. Probably the most challenging activity was to attempt and to succeed in raising $5,000 to carry on our office vocational youth organizational activities. Also, such things as club-member involvement, teamwork, and responsibility are more significant to me because of these activities.

On-the-job training for the Liberty Insurance Company, 5000 Wayzata Boulevard, St. Louis Park, Minnesota 55416, allowed me to do filing, record-keeping, and mail-room activities. Acting as relief receptionist gave me an opportunity to receive and refer callers and to act as the company's public relations ambassador.

Mr. John Jacobs, office manager for Liberty Insurance Company, and others listed on my data sheet have given me permission to use their names as references. You may call or write them for further information concerning my character and working abilities.

Will you please grant me a personal interview? You may reach me by letter or call me at (612) 937-2800 after 4:30 P.M. if you wish.

Cordially yours,

Pamela J. Eckers

Enclosure

ILLUSTRATION 2

Résumé ˋfor:
PAMELA ECKERS
3421 Texas Avenue, St. Louis Park, Minnesota 55426
(612) 937-2800

I. PERSONAL DATA
  A. Date of Birth: July 26, 1953
  B. Health: Excellent   Height: 5'4"   Weight: 115
  C. Social Security Number: 468-54-2738

II. EXPERIENCE RECORD
  A. Presently working as a records clerk and receptionist at Liberty Insurance Company, 5000 Wayzata Boulevard, St. Louis Park, Minnesota 55416. Supervisor: Nola Rowlison.
  B. Worked as a secretary during the summer of 1970 at Acme, Inc., 9200 Wayzata Boulevard, Minneapolis, Minnesota 55416. Supervisor: John Day.
  C. Worked as a kitchen aid during junior year at Texa Tonka Nursing Home, 3201 Virginia Avenue, St. Louis Park, Minnesota 55416. Supervisor: Lureen Doher.

III. EDUCATIONAL RECORD
  A. Will be graduated from St. Louis Park Senior High School, St. Louis Park, Minnesota 55426, in June, 1971.
  B. Participated in the Office Education Cooperative Part-Time Training Program in my senior year.
  C. Specialized in business courses and attained:
    1. Typewriting speed, 50 wpm; shorthand speed, 120 wpm.
    2. An understanding of transcribing machines, the IBM Magnetic Tape Selectric Typewriter, and the IBM Composer Typewriter.
    3. An understanding of good human relations between co-workers and employer-employee.
    4. A working knowledge of rotary and key-driven calculators,

ten-key adding machines, fluid duplicator, and mimeograph.
  D. Maintained a B average during my senior year.

IV. EXTRACURRICULAR RECORD
  A. Member of St. Louis Park Chapter of Minnesota Office Education Association (MOEA).
  B. Chairman of Fund Raising—responsibility of raising $5,000
for club activity.
  C. Member of Y-Teen at St. Louis Park Senior High during my
last three years.

V. REFERENCES (with permission)
  A. Mrs. Rosemary Blackstone, Office Education Coordinator, St.
Louis Park Senior High School, 6425 West 33 Street, St.
Louis Park, Minnesota 55426 (612) 929-2651.
  B. Mrs. John Lindquist, Housewife, 3433 Texas Avenue, St.
Louis Park, Minnesota 55426 (612) 937-4841.
  C. Mr. John Jacobs, Office Manager, Liberty Insurance Com-
pany, 5000 Wayzata Boulevard, St. Louis Park, Minnesota
55426 (612) 544-3101.

This type of application is appealing and inviting to read. The actual letter, or the narrative part, is of moderate length and
makes logical, psychological, and emotional appeals. The résumé is a detailed summary of data that presents a complete look
at the applicant's business and educational background; it is the
technical rather than personal part of the application. It is tabulated for eye appeal.

Of all the letters you will have to write, the letter applying for
a job will be the most important to you. Success or failure here
affects your future. Someday, someplace, you will want one job
very much. If the job is worth anything at all, there will be
other people applying for it. You will want to put your best foot
forward. You will want to look your very best. You will want to
impress the reader. You will want your request granted. "Here
comes the judge"—the real test of your letter-writing abilities.
Obviously, you will need all the skills, attitudes, and understanding necessary to fill the particular job for which you are
applying. However, just as important will be your ability to
make your letter more impressive than those of others who are

applying. "Here comes the judge" as to your ability to select the facts, interpret the facts, and set your personality in writing. "Here comes the judge" as to your ability to sell your qualifications for the job.

Get the Facts

The first step in attempting to make a job application is to accumulate facts about yourself. Of course, this should be a thorough job, so that you don't overlook anything important. Keep in mind that it will be much easier for you to cut down from a large source of facts than it will be for you to add to a skimpy supply. The résumé should include five basic categories of information:

1. Personal data
2. Educational record
3. Interests, hobbies, and achievements
4. Work experience
5. References (with permission)

It might be wise for you to take a sheet of paper or 4 x 6 cards and list as much information as you possibly can under each of these five headings. When listing this information, place the most significant facts first. This will save time when you later tabulate your résumé.

Personal Data

Data of birth, physical condition (height, weight, and general health), and social security number are listed in outline form:

1. PERSONAL DATA.
   A. Date of Birth, May 30, 1953
   B. Health: Excellent   Height: 5' 6" Weight: 125

Education

As a high school graduate, it is not necessary for you to list the elementary schools you attended. If you are to be graduated in June of the year you are writing the letter, you should say "Will be graduated from the Clinton High School, Clinton, Minnesota, on June 4, 1971." If you have already been graduated, you can say "Was graduated from the. . . ." Avoid "I will graduate" or "I graduated." Both are incorrect because only an institution has the power to graduate. As a college graduate, it is necessary for you to list the high schools and the colleges you attended. Another fact that could be included in the Education section would be any unusual overall scholastic achievement or any outstanding scholastic performance in classes that are directly related to the job for which you are applying. Also, you should indicate the performance you attained in the courses that directly relate to the job, such as in C below.

II. EDUCATIONAL RECORD
   A. Will be graduated from Clinton High School, Clinton, Minnesota, on June 4, 1971.
   B. Attained an A average in business classes.
   C. Specialized in business subjects and attained:
      1. Typewriting speed of 70 + words per minute.
      2. Shorthand speed of 140 words per minute.
      3. Understanding of the following business machines: dictaphone, stencil duplicator, electric typewriter, IBM Magnetic Tape Selectric Typewriter, IBM Composer Typewriter.
   D. Have been accepted by the College of Saint Catherine, St. Paul, Minnesota 55102.

Also, be sure to list any special honors or awards, such as the honor roll, the National Honor Society, achievement awards, honor student recognition, and so on.

If you are listing more than one school which you have attended (not counting elementary schools), place them in chronological order with the most recent school listed last. *This vio-*

lates the general rule of listing as to order of importance for the other major headings.

Extracurricular Activities and Interests

Most employers like to see some evidence of a well-rounded individual, one who is compatible with others and has a good attitude toward leadership.

Actually, there are two types of activities available to students: (1) Co-curricular—those that are related directly to classroom instruction or discipline and that motivate a field of instruction, like the vocational youth organizations (OEA, DECA, FBLA, VICA, FFA, and FHA). (2) Extracurricular—those not directly related to the classroom instruction or discipline (sports, chorus, debate, and so on). See the following example:

III. INTERESTS, HOBBIES, AND ACHIEVEMENTS
    A. Vice president of the Clinton Chapter of MOEA
    B. Student secretary for Office Coordinator
    C. Member of Donaldson's Teen Board
    D. Junior volunteer at Methodist Hospital
    E. Member of 1970 School Yearbook staff
    F. Hobbies of skiing and reading

Work Experience Record

Many of you may have already accumulated work experience. In any event, to have gathered work experience before being graduated from high school is substantial and impressive.

Make a survey of your work experience. List each entry, beginning with your most recent position. Be sure to include job or jobs held, employer or company name, address, and supervisor's name, such as:

IV. WORK EXPERIENCE RECORD
    A. Presently working as a secretary at Northern Propane Gas Company, 4820 Excelsior Boulevard, St. Louis Park, Minnesota 55416. Supervisor: Mr. LeRoy Lindbloom, Engineer.

    B. Worked as a clerk the summer of 1968 at Woolworth's, Knollwood Plaza, St. Louis Park, Minnesota 55426. Supervisor: Mr. Allen Yoder, Manager.

List of References

Consider two or three references *other than relatives* who can speak well of you. Get permission from them to use their names as references before listing them. If the person you ask is quick to accept, you can usually assume that he'll give you a good reference.

Employers usually place great importance on the recommendations made by people who have seen your job performance; therefore, be sure to include at least one and preferably two past employers. It is also wise to list at least one member of your school staff, as employers invariably check at your school regarding your school record. Don't include more than one personal or character reference. When listing your references, be sure to include their complete names, describe their positions, give their business addresses and telephone numbers. Make it as easy as possible for the person reading your qualifications to contact your references, such as:

V. REFERENCES (with permission)
    A. Mr. LeRoy Lindbloom, Engineering Manager, Northern Propane Gas Company, 4820 Excelsior Boulevard, St. Louis Park, Minnesota 55416 (612) 927-9981.
    B. Mr. Allen Yoder, Manager, Woolworth's, 8402 Highway 7, St. Louis Park, Minnesota 55426 (612) 938-1170.

Once you have compiled a listing of all your qualifications and have double-checked to see that you "got all the facts" and included all pertinent information, you are ready to summarize these qualifications for your application letter. Such a summary is called a data sheet or résumé.

Write the Facts

The data sheet or résumé, to be effective, must be tabulated in good form so it is attractive. You must arrange information according to importance. It should be well organized and give an orderly presentation.

Individually type each data sheet on 8½ x 11, 20-pound bond paper or reproduce it by offset or commercial printing. Never use a carbon copy!

The format for the résumé or data sheet should begin with a well-displayed heading containing such personal details as name, address, and telephone number. Then you must decide upon the overall sequence. As already stated, the order should be from the most important to the least important.

It is up to you to choose a one- or two-page data sheet; however, one page is preferred. Limiting yourself to one page forces you to reevaluate your facts and delete irrelevant material. Just as lengthy letters are burdensome, so are lengthy data sheets. If, however, you feel you *must* have a two-page data sheet to include all your qualifications, use two sheets.

For eye appeal, use ample space, clear-cut headings for main groups of data, and subheads. Use parallel phrasing in listing items such as:

III. INTERESTS, HOBBIES, AND ACHIEVEMENTS
    A. Member of Minnesota Chapter of DVC
    B. Student secretary for Office Coordinator
    C. Member of Donaldson's Teen Board
    D. Editor of 1971 School Yearbook

Use words and phrases rather than sentences, since they are easier to read and to review.

Previously a place was left on the résumé for the applicant's photograph to be attached; however, because states—in their fair-employment laws—and Congress—in its 1964 enactment of Title VII of the Civil Rights Act—say that employers cannot discriminate because of color, race, religion, or sex, it seems to be in better taste not to include a photograph.

This well-prepared and complete data sheet or résumé may serve another purpose. If you ever apply for a job by telephone or in person and company policy does not require a letter of application, you can bring a data sheet with you to the interview. When you introduce yourself to the interviewer, you could say: "Hello, Mr. Brown. I'm Betty Smith making application for the secretarial vacancy in the research lab. I've compiled this résumé. Maybe it can be of some assistance to you in our interview."

The first step in writing the letter of application, then, is to use 4 x 6 cards to "get all the facts" you can about yourself. Use one or more cards for each main head as suggested previously.

After you have rechecked them to make sure you haven't forgotten any pertinent information, use these cards to set up a complete, well-presented, attractive data sheet. Try to limit it to one page, but make it "chuck-full" of interesting tidbits about yourself. An applicant with a short listing of qualifications may indicate that he is actually short of qualifications! So "get all the facts" and you've taken the first right step in writing this important letter.

Whip Up a Really Good Letter

After you have decided on the job you would like to have, you should make an all-out effort to learn as much as you can about it and the *firm*. (Can you imagine anyone wanting to apply for a job about which he doesn't know such general facts as location of the firm, job requirements, salary range, opportunity for advancement, and so on?) This type of preliminary investigation can be made by a brief telephone call to the company's personnel office (if practical in terms of distance), face-to-face conversation with an employee of the firm, or a thorough reading of the job advertisement (some of these thoroughly describe the job at hand). Your local library or employment agencies can be of assistance in providing such information.

To write a *really* good letter, the more preliminary investigating you do, the better opportunity you will have to sell your product—you. A blind approach to a job application can be as unsuccessful as attempting to sell a product to a public about which you know nothing. How can you write persuasively and make logical, psychological, and emotional appeals unless you know your market—your prospective employer and the firm he represents? Any attempt you make to learn something about your prospective employer and his firm will be easily recognized and credited to your initiative as a desirable characteristic for any prospective employee.

With this type of information, as well as an effective and attractive résumé typed and ready to be attached, you are prepared to write a really good sales letter—your letter of application. "Here comes the judge," the real test of your letter-writing abilities.

It is necessary then that you write a descriptive, explanatory, and highly persuasive letter. "Getting the facts" for your résumé forced you to accumulate much information about yourself. Getting the preliminary facts about the job, your prospective employer, and the firm he represents has armed you with information concerning the requirements of the position that you are seeking. All this vital information will help you to make the *match*—the match between the job requirements and your qualifications.

If the letter makes such a match obvious to your reader, you will be considered for an interview. After all, you are in demand. The employer needs you if you can do the job. Your résumé can serve as the job qualification fact sheet; however, it should be your *letter* that will sell your prospective employer on the fact that you have the qualifications necessary to fill his job needs. The match must be made *obvious;* it cannot be left to chance. You must tell him how the various qualifications you possess actually meet the requirements of the job he is attempting to fill.

Employers are aware of the significant Work Adjustment Theory, which is in essence a "happy marriage" between the employee's interests, aptitudes, and personality and the job's significant activities, requirements, and technical and environmental factors. Yes, the employer is vitally interested in this *match* because he knows that profits are a result of maximum production and that maximum production is the result of capable employees who are happy with what they are doing.

Thus, you must sell your reader—the prospective employer—on your product—you. In the letter of application, match your qualifications to his needs. With this approach, you are bound to land the job. He can't afford *not* to hire you.

"Here Comes the Judge" Letter Format

Will you succeed in convincing your prospective employer that you are the best person for the job? "Here comes the judge" —your letter. Try to persuade him by using the following four-step letter format. Remember that your data sheet is attached to the letter and should be referred to throughout the letter. Consistently lead the reader into the data sheet for actual facts.

1. Establish contact (or attract favorable attention) by:
   a. Taking pains with the physical appearance and arrangement of the letter material (stationery, typing, paragraphing, grammar, punctuation, spelling, and so on).

    b. Explaining how the vacancy became known.
    c. Indicating the exact purpose of the letter:

Mr. John Barret, my principal, has informed me of a salesman vacancy in your firm. Will you please consider me an applicant?

 2. Create desire or interest by:
    a. Stating and then analyzing the major requirements of the position in mind.
    b. Showing conclusively that your education, training, and experience meet these requirements specifically.
 3. Convince the employer that you are the person for the job by:
    a. Supplementing the statement already made with a presentation of those personal qualifications or characteristics which seem most desirable.

During my senior year, I was elected vice president of the Clinton Chapter of the MDVC. Working to gain the support and team effort of my peers has made me conscious of the importance of good human relationships. This awareness should make me a more qualified and perceptive salesman.

    b. Manifesting genuine interest in his business, together with an expression of confidence in your ability to adapt your particular training to meet the employer's requirements.
    c. Suggesting, if it seems appropriate, your ultimate aim, as well as your immediate objective.
    d. Reassuring the employer that you don't just want work, but rather the chance to tackle a given problem and solve it.
 4. Simulate action by:
    a. Offering references that will vouch for your experience, education, and character.
    b. Requesting an interview.
    c. Supplying the employer with the necessary information for him to arrange the interview.

The Beginning

The first paragraph of the letter of application should arouse the immediate attention of the reader. If the letter fails here, it usually fails in its ultimate purpose—to get you an interview. Most employers judge the ability of an applicant by the degree of excellence of his letter in both expression and organization.

The beginning should reveal the purpose of your letter and indicate where or how you learned about the position. Begin directly rather than vaguely. Do not leave it to the reader to guess the purpose of your letter. Although your first paragraph should suggest your individuality by avoiding trite, hackneyed beginnings, it should not be too radical, eccentric, or artificial.

1. Assuming that you have read an ad about the job in today's *Times,* consider the following introductory sentence:

Will you please consider my application for the accountant vacancy in your firm as advertised in today's June 1 *New York Times.*

I was graduated with a B.A. in Accounting from the University of Missouri last June.

2. Assuming that a friend—not known to the reader—told you about the job, consider the following introductory sentence:

Mr. John Edwards, a friend of mine who has worked as an accountant for 22 years and encouraged me to pursue this career, has suggested that I apply for an accounting job at your office. Will you please consider me an applicant.

While obtaining my degree in Accounting from Miller's Business School, I worked part-time for Mr. Edwards as an accounting clerk.

3. Assuming that a friend of yours—an expert in your field, well known to the reader and highly respected by him—told you about the job, consider the following introductory sentence:

A personal friend, Mr. Harold Bisel, a well-known certified public accountant in the Twin Cities, has encouraged me to apply for the accountant's position in your firm. Will you please consider my application.

My schooling at the University of Maine and my work experience for Mr. Bisel have provided me with valuable knowledge of the field of public accounting.

The Middle

The arrangement of the middle paragraphs of your letter depends upon the requirements of the position and your age, education, and experience.

The middle, or the body of your letter, may be conveniently divided under the following headings. You will, of course, place your best selling points in the most prominent position.

1. An analysis of the prospective employer's business, or a presentation of the particular requirements of the position.

2. A detailed account of your education and your practical work experience.

3. A convincing statement showing the relationship between your particular qualifications and the specific requirements of the position. This is the match we discussed, and is probably the most important part of your letter as it shows why you have an interest in the position.

4. A presentation of personal data. This material is of utmost importance to the application. Nowhere in your letter are you afforded a better opportunity to reveal your innermost self— your ambition, your determination, your ability to overcome difficulties and see them through to a successful finish. These and other positive traits of character are what the employer is looking for. Interests and hobbies often describe you better than anything else you may say.

The body of the letter should not be too long or involved.

Each paragraph should emphasize a particular selling point. Sentences should be clear and to the point. Avoid all irrelevant material, yet do not allow any breaks or gaps to appear in the record of your education or experience.

The End

The end or conclusion of your letter of application has a two-fold purpose—to request an interview and to make it easy for the reader to grant the interview. Leave no doubt in the reader's mind of your desire for an interview. State definitely and completely how and when he may reach you. Give as much attention to the individuality and the force of your ending as you do to the beginning of your letter.

Pam's letter, illustrated on page 144, is outlined as follows:

1. The beginning—job application.
2. The middle—educational record, work experience record, reference listing.
3. The end—request for interview.

Notice how Pam consistently led her reader into her data sheet, as in the third paragraph: "As you will notice on my enclosed data sheet . . . ," and in the fifth paragraph: "Mr. John Jacobs, office manager for Liberty Insurance Company, and others listed on my data sheet. . . ."

Waiting for the Verdict

While waiting for the verdict—did you get the job or didn't you?—only a few applicants think to write a letter thanking the employer for the interview. Employment people frankly admit that they are impressed when they receive this type of letter and that they don't receive enough of them. Obviously, you probably won't be considered for the job *just* because you remembered to write such a letter, but it could have some bearing on a very close contest between two applicants.

This letter is a just plain "being nice" letter. All it needs is to be prompt, sincere, and unified. It should be written on the same day as the interview or no later than the day following the interview. It should reach the reader before he has made a decision. Appreciation for such things as being called in for an interview (not the time spent in the interview), and extra courtesies like touring the firm, lunch, or an introduction to executives should be expressed sincerely. Avoid being gushy and do not overuse superlatives. You may end the letter by expressing your desire to hear from the reader.

The following is an example of a follow-up letter:

Thank you for allowing me to talk to you in person regarding my qualifications for the secretarial position in your research department.

Also, I certainly appreciated meeting your president, Mr. Davidson. It is understandable why your firm has enjoyed such success.

This experience made me even more eager to be employed with you and to learn of your decision.

In conclusion, it is wise to re-emphasize the importance of writing really good letters of application. It's as simple as this: The letter of application is your opportunity to "get your foot in the door." Don't let your reader shut the door in your face like this superintendent did when he read the following two letters from teaching applicants. They have been salvaged from his rejection file (the wastepaper basket) for negative appraisal only. They make a couple of well-qualified people sound very unqualified and unworthy of consideration, don't they?

April 10, 19—

Mr. R. D. Sullivan, Superintendent
Tacoma Public Schools, District 2
Maxwell Avenue East
Tacoma, Washington 99206

Your next Shop
Teacher opening,
Mr. Sullivan,

may find you asking yourself these questions:
WHERE CAN I GET AN EXPERIENCED SHOP TEACHER . . .
    . . . who ENJOYS WORKING with students?
    . . . who is CO-OPERATIVE with Administration and faculty?
    . . . who takes an ACTIVE INTEREST in all school activities?
    . . . who gets the MAXIMUM USE out of all shop equipment?
    . . . who has CONTINUED his professional STUDIES?
    . . . who will become PART of the COMMUNITY?
As these questions come up, Mr. Sullivan, look for the ANSWERS
on the next pages.

Sincerely,

Claude Riversons
14 Stone Street
Tacoma, Washington 99216
Phone: 523-8361

Ladies and Gentlemen:

From an education in Rhetoric and History, Foreign Language and
English, Library Management and training, Journalism, mathematics,
and Science, kinds not atomic such as Physics or Chemistry, also Education travel and geography, Psychology, Graduate School advancement etc. I have a certificate to teach and reissued again this year
some 12 to 13 yrs. after my first Middleton Filing Experience in
which job I successfully finished my library practice work. Choose
any four to assign me to; then write to me to come to sign the schools
contract please for the work to which you can appoint or elect me to
do competent work for:

1. Plane Geometry?
2. Ancient History?
3. Home Economics
   Projects?
4. Biology?

5. Art Appreciation
   and Arts Con-
   structions
6. Music and Art
   Appreciation?

7. United States His-
   tory and Cur-
   rent Events
8. English I and II?

9. English III and	some extracur-	guage Choices
IV?	ricular recrea-	of Latin, Ger-
10. Phys. Educ. Girls	tion	man, French,
Only? and	11. Foreign Lan-	Spanish

I will answer promptly all written offers granting work assignments at whatever salary you found you intend to offer below Superintendent Rank and Rank of Principal in Charge below Superintendency. I have 3 yrs. experience in assistant Principal work and I like the position. Also I enjoy beginning as instructor of grade 8 if there are not good highschool vacancies for me at present.

Sincerely and respectfully,

Reverse the Decision

Another employment letter that you may have to write for yourself or your employer is the resignation letter. The resignation letter, or the letter that reverses the judge's decision, should:

1. Be brief and to the point.

2. State the date of termination.

3. State the reasons for terminating employment. (You should use tact in stating reasons. For instance, you should not say "I am taking a position with the Smith Company because they pay more money." "Personal advancement" is one acceptable reason that is noncommittal.)

4. Mention that working with the company has been enjoyable. Say this in a sentence or two.

5. Use "respectfully yours" as a complimentary close.

The following is an example of a letter of resignation:

Please accept my resignation as executive secretary for the Research Department effective June 10, 1971.

Since I plan to be married and move to Denver, Colorado, on July 1, I will need a few weeks to get things ready and packed. If you wish, I will be happy to train my replacement.

Thank you for the opportunity to work with your Research Department. This job trained me to exercise common sense and thus become a more perceptive secretary. My replacement has much to look forward to!

Respectfully yours,

18

Size It Up

In the world of today, you would be remiss if you did not concern yourself with report writing. Reports that "size up" situations and bring back the facts are common and can be done orally or in writing. Our interest here is the written report.

Actually, there are two basic types of reports: the informal and the formal. The informal report is usually one that is developed without strict adherence to rules and format; the formal report is usually developed according to definite rules and follows a standard format. An excellent example of a formal report in its final appearance is a thesis.

If you will then visualize the report as an effort to "size up" the situation and to deliver information to someone who is in need of it (this includes your superiors, co-workers, fellow club members, and sometimes the public in general), you will recognize that the traditional or scientific method of solving problems plays an important part in business report writing.

First of all, you must define your problem and state it in the title of your report. Secondly, you should gather the facts that will be needed to reach a solution. This could mean examining past records, conducting experiments, interviewing people, and probably consulting existing literature. Next, you should analyze the data collected. Obviously, such things as sorting, coding or classifying, computing, and tabulating are common activities in this step. Finally, on the basis of careful evaluation, you should select the alternative that appears to be the best solution. All these steps must be taken before you are ready to draft your report.

Business report writing is similar to business letter writing. Both must be fitted to your reader's needs, although the letter demands more writing that is reader-oriented. Both must be accurate and easy to read. Readability is harder to achieve in report writing than in business letter writing.

As an employee, you may be faced with the problem of preparing periodic reports or progress reports. This will mean either writing information reports, which merely present facts, or compiling the more sophisticated analytical reports. In a report that analyzes, you will be required to interpret the facts for the reader and in some instances to suggest a remedy or remedies to a problem.

Size It Up Informally

The most popular report that you may be asked to write is the simpler, less complicated informal report. The distinguishing characteristic of this report is its physical appearance. The informal report can be compared with the informal theme—a set of rules and procedures is not often required in these reports; and the formal report can be compared with the formal thesis—a title page, table of contents, bibliography, index, and so on, are almost always required in these reports.

"Sizing it up informally," or informal report writing, is most common when research is light and where content is brief. The three most common informal reports that many of us may be asked to write are the letter or memo report, news release, or minutes of meetings.

The memorandum appears below.

The letter report contains all the elements of a regular business letter—heading, inside address, salutation, body, closing, and signature.

When you prepare an informal report, either a letter, memo, news release, or minutes of meetings, you should make a continuous flow of the text. Or, if it is too lengthy or cumbersome, you may wish to attach separate sheets to the report in the form of enclosures. The following office memorandum is an example of the continuous-flow approach. It will also be your prerogative to use a personal tone or a more impersonal (third person) tone. The personal tone, however, seems to be preferred.

INTER-OFFICE MEMORANDUM · THE McKINNEY COMPANY
TO   Secretaries, Stenographers, and Typists
FROM   William Fowler—Communications
DATE   July 16, 19___
SUBJECT   Wire Service Schedule

                          Effective September 1, 19___

    Company Offices

Teletype service is available to the company offices listed below and on the following page.

Messages to these offices don't require a complete address. You need show only the name of the addressee and the code letter for the office. Before you code a wire, check to see if the addressee is at this location.

Office	Teletype Code	Time Zone	Office Hours
Avon	AV	CDT	8:00–4:30
Lodi	LOD	PDT	8:00–4:30
Ogden	OGA	MDT	8:00–4:30
Toledo	TL	EDT	8:00–4:30
Vallajo	VLA	PDT	8:00–4:30

If you have any questions regarding wire service, please call us.

                                            Cordially yours,

AM

Whether you choose a letter or the memorandum, you will have to decide also how you will reason your explanation. If you recall in Lesson 2, in developing your letter-writing skills, you were exposed to an explanation of inductive and deductive reasoning. Whether you were conscious of it or not, you have been developing inductive and deductive reasoning throughout this book. For example, when you could say "yes" to a letter of request, you were told to give them the good news first and then do the explaining. When you had to say "no" to a special request, you were told to first explain the reasons and then come to your refusal as a conclusion. Wasn't the procedure for developing the "yes" letter really an example of deductive reasoning and the procedure for developing the "no" letter really an example of inductive reasoning? Inductive reasoning is really a persuasive approach, presenting adequate information before drawing a conclusion or making a recommendation. Deductive reasoning, in essence, is making a conclusion or recommendation and then presenting facts and information to support it. Both processes or sequences can be used effectively in informal report writing; however, the "no" letter, or deductive reasoning, approach seems to be preferred.

Whether you write a letter, memo, news release, or minutes of meetings, you will also have to decide how you are going to present your methods and findings. You may wish to present these findings in alphabetical order, in order of importance (news release), reverse order of importance, or in chronological order (minutes of meetings), whichever serves your purpose best.

News Releases

You will want to select the most important or unusual aspect of the message and stress that point in the introduction of your news release. Just as in letter writing, "getting to the point" is an important rule to follow when writing news releases.

Headings

The heading for a news release should be brief, descriptive, and grammatically correct. Avoid trying to be clever or daring. Many writers confuse such attempts with style or creativity; however, most editors are not fooled.

Mechanics in Preparing the News Release

The release should be typed, double-spaced, if possible. If not, a clear, neatly handwritten copy may be written in ink. It should be on a good quality 8½ x 11 bond paper with 1-inch side margins and a 1½-inch bottom margin. A specially prepared blocked letterhead is typed at the left top margin, 1-inch from the top edge of the paper; it includes the word From:, the name of the sender, his title, his address, and his telephone number. Also, on the first line of the heading, the date is typed at the right margin.

It is important to type the release information in caps, such as: FOR IMMEDIATE RELEASE or FOR RELEASE: MONDAY, JANUARY 30, 19__.

If the news release is longer than one page in length, the word MORE is typed at the lower right corner, two spaces below the last line of the release, and all succeeding pages are numbered at the center. The last page of the release is noted by centering and typing -30- or # # # # two spaces after the last typed line.

The following example of a news release reports facts to its readers.

From: Mary L. Bilinkas   December 28, 19__
       Coordinator Information & Events
       County College of Morris
       Route 10 & Center Grove Road
       Dover, NJ 07801

FOR IMMEDIATE RELEASE

RANDOLPH TWP.—Man and computer—the miracle machine—are combining at County College of Morris to produce skilled typists more rapidly.

Officials of Sunny Hill Publishing Company and CCM students of Robert D. Applegate, CCM data processing chairman, are the major components in an experiment designed to shorten teaching procedures in secretarial science.

Sunny Hill's Dr. Alvin Ludd and Dr. John Davidson watched recently as students Edward Jones, Jack Stacy, and Donna Flynn ran a series of programs designed to study typewriter word analysis.

The programs performed in 6½ minutes the equivalent of 30 hours of a typist's calculations.

Typewriting word analysis was the subject of Dr. Davidson's doctoral dissertation at Syracuse College. With Mr. Applegate and Mrs. Mary Rose serving as Sunny Hill consultants, it was only natural that CCM should be called on to lend a bit of know-how in preparing a special computer program that was six months in the making.

MORE

What the program actually does is provide an analysis of the physical strokes and motions involved in typing, in order to reduce the teaching of the subject to a science. The program also is aimed at reducing the number of hours a typing student spends in learning the skill.

According to Mr. Applegate, it is estimated that this computer analysis and its application may reduce the learning time for the average typing student by as much as 25 percent.

"Our ultimate goal," he said, "is to involve the typing student with computer analysis. We've been working on this program for six months preparing computer programs that will handle a basic vocabulary of 10,000 words. Once completed," he added, "the study could be the basis for a breakthrough in the present typing teaching system."

CCM may play a vital role in the future of the program. Discussion is underway concerning the possibility of County College of Morris operating a pilot program to supplement Sunny Hill's efforts.

The program would involve the secretarial science department and data processing technology areas of the college faculty.

-30-

Minutes of a Meeting

Nearly everyone will sooner or later become involved in reporting minutes of a meeting—be it civic, social, church, or business. Although a rather common responsibility, this job requires the utmost accuracy and is a serious responsibility.

The minutes of a meeting are the record of what has happened at the meeting and include the following data:

1) Date, time, place, and presiding officers of meeting
2) Attendance record
3) Approval or correction of the previous minutes
4) Approval or correction of the treasurer's report (with report attached to the minutes)
5) Unfinished business carried from last meeting and acted upon at the present
6) Reports (summarized only—not verbatim)
7) New business (main motions and resolutions)
8) Committee appointments
9) Election of officers
10) Adjournment

Main Motions

Main motions must be recorded, and such information as the name of the person making the motion, the exact wording of the motion, the person seconding the motion, and the result of the vote must be included in the minutes. The motion for adjournment does not require its exact wording to be recorded.

Mechanics of Recording the Minutes

As illustrated in the example on page 170, minutes are written or typed double-spaced in the past tense and in the order in which the events occurred.

The heading includes the group, date, and kind of meeting in capital letters. It is followed by the first paragraph, which includes the date, time, place, and presiding officer.

Names of attending and absent members are listed alphabetically.

Resolutions are indented five spaces on both sides, single-spaced if typed, and the word WHEREAS is typed in capital letters. The following example is a resolution of congratulations:

RESOLUTION

Adopted February 10, 19__

WHEREAS, the Junior Red Cross of Morris County helps the youth of the county find expression and interest; and

WHEREAS, the success of this organization is largely due to the leadership of its advisor, Miss Janet Hughes, Personnel Director for the Swantes Manufacturing Company; therefore be it

RESOLVED, that the members of this organization go on record as expressing their congratulations and best wishes to Miss Hughes and that the secretary present a copy of this resolution to Miss Hughes in the name of the Board of Directors of the Vantage Corporation of Minneapolis.

THE COUNTY COLLEGE OF MORRIS
OFFICE EDUCATION ASSOCIATION MEETING
NOVEMBER 23, 19__

The monthly meeting of the County College of Morris Office Education Association was called to order by President Cathy Potoczak on Friday, November 23, 19__, at 12:00 noon.

A quorum was present as all members were in attendance except David Andrews, Mary Beth Davidson, and Joanne Hutton.

Copies of the minutes of the October 20 meeting were distributed by the secretary. Since there were no additions or corrections, the minutes were approved.

Copies of the treasurer's report were distributed by the treasurer, Bonnie Wachter. No corrections were made, so the report was approved.

Fund Raising Committee Report

Chairman of the Fund Raising Committee, Janice Wong, reported that Nestle Candy could be bought on consignment, and that a forty percent profit return could be earned, and that if an order was placed by Friday, October 30, the club could benefit from the Christmas buying.

Much discussion pro and con to candy selling resulted from the report. It was moved by Jan Wong and seconded by Betty Edwards to have the Fund Raising Committee place an order for 200 cases of Nestle Chocolate Crunch on consignment to be delivered before November 30.

It was unanimously carried.

Since there was no further new business, the meeting was adjourned at 1:30 p.m.

Respectfully submitted,

———————————————
Brenda Moss, Secretary

Size It Up Formally

You will also be asked to "size up" a situation and report it formally, which means you will follow a standard formula when you draft the report. The formal report will be used when the problem is complicated and time is not a deciding factor, when you wish to impress your reader with organization and orderliness, when the text is lengthy, when you wish to have a formal style of writing (although a formal style may be used in an informal report), or when you wish to use an impersonal third-person tone (however, many businessmen demand a personal "you" or "I" tone because of its interest value).

Some people prefer the formal report because, if it is a relatively long report, they can expect it to be divided into the following parts.

Title Page

This is the first page of the formal report and usually includes four things: the title, the name of the person receiving the report, the author, and the date of completion. Of course, all of these things should be arranged attractively. Never number a title page. The title is usually centered in capital letters and should be as concise as possible. If more than one line is required for the title, the lines should be arranged in an inverted pyramid style, such as:

A COMPARATIVE ANALYSIS OF THE DUTIES
OF THE CLERK AND THE SECRETARY

Letter of Transmittal

This follows the title page and should not be numbered. It should follow any good letter-writing style and may or may not be typed on letterhead. It varies in length and actually says "I have 'sized it up' and here is the report you asked me to prepare."

Preface

The preface, sometimes referred to as "the part that only the author is interested in," is an introductory discussion. It should include what the reader cannot find in the text. An author may use a preface to give background material, or reasons for undertaking the project, and the method of conducting his research.

A Roman numeral is used to number the preface page.

Table of Contents

This is a list of what will follow in the text of the report. Items included in the table of contents are numbered with the page on which that item begins and sometimes where it ends. Roman numerals are also used on the page or pages containing the table of contents.

List of Illustrations

The list of illustrations helps the reader locate visual and graphic aids by listing the page numbers on which they appear. Again, a Roman numeral is used to number this page.

Synopsis

The synopsis is a summary of the text. Length is a matter of choice, but it should include a statement of the problem, your findings, and your conclusions or recommendations. The purpose of placing the summary before the actual text is to briefly relay the message of the report to your reader. This section ends the Roman numeral series.

Body or Text

This is the main section of the formal report. It is here the subject is explained and analyzed. An introduction, including a statement of the purpose and perhaps the methods used in gathering facts, opens the body of the report. This is followed by discussion, analysis, and a presentation of the facts. A conclusion or summary ends this part of the report.

The first page of the body or text marks the beginning of a second series of page numbers. Arabic numbers should be used and will continue through the supplementary sections of the appendix, bibliography, and index which follow. Remember the manuscript rules of never numbering the first page of the text.

Appendix

This supplementary section contains graphic aids that would be too cumbersome if inserted in the body of the report. However, reference to them should be made in the report. Material that is less than one-half of a page should be included in the text rather than in the appendix. The reader should not be asked to flip to the appendix for constant reference.

Bibliography

The bibliography is a list of books and periodicals used as sources of information. Follow good form by including the author's name, the title of the article, the name of the book or periodical, volume and issue number, name of the publisher, place of publication, and the date of publication. This listing should be in alphabetical order by authors' surnames.

Index

The index is the final supplementary section and is an alphabetical listing of all the significant names, topics, and subtopics contained in the report, together with a notation of the pages on which each appears throughout the report.

The format or the detailed characteristics of the formal report will require decision making on your part. For example, you may center the page numbers or put them at the right margin. Whatever format you choose, be consistent.

Reference Section

It is expected that all the business communications that you write will be correctly worded and punctuated according to the accepted rules of the English language. If you fail to give proper attention to these routine rules of writing, your ideas—no matter how creative or convincing—may fail in their purpose.

This reference section is a condensed summary of those sections of Gavin and Sabin's *Reference Manual for Stenographers and Typists*, Fourth Edition,* that represent common problems facing the business letter writer. You may wish to refer to the manual for a thorough coverage of grammar, punctuation, and so on.

Punctuation

The Period

1. Use a period to mark the end of a sentence that makes a statement or expresses a command.

* Ruth E. Gavin and William A. Sabin, *Reference Manual for Stenographers and Typists*, 4th ed., Gregg Division, McGraw-Hill Book Company, New York, 1970.

I was very happy to hear about your promotion. (Statement)
Be sure to answer Mrs. Andrews' letter promptly. (Command)

2. Use a period to mark the end of an indirect question.

The only question I have is whether the job will be completed on schedule.
Who the new vice president will be has not yet been decided.

The Question Mark

1. Use a question mark at the end of a direct question.

Where are the records for Frasier, Inc.?
Why not see your dealer today?

2. Use a question mark at the end of a sentence that is phrased like a statement but spoken with the rising intonation of a question.

They still doubt his ability?
These figures are correct?

3. A series of brief questions at the end of a sentence may be separated by commas or (for emphasis) by question marks. Do not capitalize the individual questions.

Can you estimate the cost of the roofing, the tile work, and the painting?
or: Can you estimate the cost of the roofing? the tile work? the painting?

4. A question mark enclosed in parentheses may be used to express doubt or uncertainty about a word or phrase within a sentence.

He was graduated from Oberlin in 1942(?).

The Exclamation Point

1. Use an exclamation point at the end of a sentence (or an expression that stands for a sentence) to indicate enthusiasm, surprise, incredulity, urgency, or strong feeling.

Yes! Dresses, jackets, and coats are selling at 50 percent off!

2. A single word may be followed by an exclamation point to express intense feeling. The sentence that follows it is punctuated as usual.

Wait! We can't let that mistake pass.

3. When such words are repeated for emphasis, an exclamation point follows each repetition.

Hush! Hush! Don't let our competitors hear this.

The Comma

The comma has two primary functions: it *separates* elements within a sentence whose relationship to one another would otherwise be unclear, and it *sets off* parenthetical elements that interrupt the flow of thought from subject to verb to object or complement. It takes only a single comma to "separate," but it typically requires two commas to "set off."

1. *In Compound Sentences.* When a compound sentence consists of two independent clauses joined by *and, but, or,* or *nor,* a "separating" comma should precede the conjunction.

Judson spoke for twenty minutes, *and* then he answered questions from the audience.
The material in this dress is not the right color, *nor* is it the quality ordered.

2. If the two clauses of a compound sentence are short, the comma may be omitted before the conjunction.

Their prices are low and they offer good service.
Please initial these forms and return them by Monday.

3. *In Complex Sentences.* A complex sentence contains one independent clause and one or more dependent clauses. *After, although, as, because, before, if, since, unless, when,* and *while* are among the words most frequently used to introduce dependent clauses.

4. When a dependent clause *precedes* a main clause, separate the two clauses with a comma.

Before we can make a decision, we must have all the facts.

5. When a dependent clause *follows* the main clause or *falls within* the main clause, commas are used or omitted depending on whether the dependent clause is essential (restrictive) or nonessential (nonrestrictive).

a. An *essential* clause is necessary to the meaning of the sentence. Because it *cannot be omitted,* it should not be set off by commas.

This ruling applies to everyone *who works in the plant.* (Tells which persons.)
Tom said *that he would wait.* (Tells what was said.)

b. A *nonessential* clause provides additional descriptive or explanatory detail. Because it *can be omitted* without changing the meaning of the sentence, it should be set off by commas.

He stopped off in Chicago to see his father, *who is an eminent lawyer.* (Simply adds information about the father.)

c. A dependent clause occurring within a sentence must always be set off by commas when it interrupts the flow of the sentence.

I can set up the meeting for tomorrow or, *if that is inconvenient,* for Friday.

6. *With Participial, Infinitive, and Prepositional Phrases.* Use a comma after an *introductory participial phrase.*

Speaking in a loud voice, the chairman called the meeting to order.

7. Use a comma after an *introductory infinitive phrase* unless the phrase is the subject of the sentence. (Infinitive phrases are introduced by the word *to.*)

To obtain the best results from the camera, follow these directions.

8. Use a comma after an *introductory prepositional phrase* unless the phrase is short and no misunderstanding is likely to result from the omission of the comma.

In response to the many requests of our customers, we are opening a suburban branch. (Comma required after a long phrase.)

9. *With Introductory, Parenthetical, or Transitional Expressions.* Use commas to set off parenthetical elements—that is, words, phrases, or clauses that are not necessary to the completeness of the structure or the meaning of the sentence. Such expressions either provide a transition from one thought to the next or reflect the writer's attitude toward the meaning of the sentence.

After all, you have done more for him than he had any right to expect.
It is generally understood, *however,* that he will accept the position.

10. *In a Series.* When the last member of a series of three or more items is preceded by *and*, *or*, or *nor*, place a comma before the conjunction as well as between the other items.

Study the rules for the use of the comma, the semicolon, *and* the colon.

11. *With Adjectives.* When two or more consecutive adjectives modify the same noun, separate the adjectives by commas.

The employer described him as a quiet, *efficient* worker. (A worker who is quiet and efficient.)

12. *With Identifying Appositive or Explanatory Expressions.* Words, phrases, and clauses that identify or explain other terms should be set off by commas.

Mr. Clark, *the president,* is retiring on Monday, *June 30.*

13. *With Interruptions of Thought and Afterthoughts.* Use commas to set off words, phrases, or clauses that interrupt the flow of a sentence or that are loosely added at the end as an afterthought.

She has received, *so I was told,* a letter of commendation from the mayor.
The exhibit contained only modern art, *if I remember correctly.*

14. *To Indicate Omitted Words.* Use a comma to indicate the omission of a word or words that are clearly understood from the context. (The omitted words are usually verbs.)

The English test was given to all students; the history test, to a selected group.

15. *In Direct Address.* Names and titles used in direct address must be set off by commas.

You cannot deny, *Mr. Monroe,* that you made that statement.

16. *In Dates.* Use two commas to set off the year when it follows the month and day or the month alone.

He began work on January 2, 1970, under the terms of the contract.

17. *With States and Countries.* Use two commas to set off the name of a state, a country, a county, etc., that directly follows a city name.

You can fly from Miami, *Florida,* to Bogotá, *Colombia,* in under four hours.

18. *With* Jr., Sr., *Etc.* Use commas to set off designations following a person's name, such as *Jr., Sr., Esq.,* and abbreviations signifying academic degrees or religious orders.

Mr. L. B. Kelly, *Jr.,* sailed for Europe today. (A growing trend in business correspondence is to omit the commas with *Jr.* and *Sr.*) We were represented in court by Henry E. Stevens, *Esq.,* of New York.

19. *With* Inc. *and* Ltd. Insert a comma before *Inc.* and *Ltd.* in company names unless you know that the official name of the company is written without a comma. Within a sentence, a comma must follow the abbreviation if a comma also precedes it.

Field Hats, Ltd.   BUT: Time Inc.

20. *In Figures.* When numbers run to four or more figures, use commas to separate thousands, hundreds of thousands, millions, etc.

$2,375.88   147,300

21. Do not use commas in year numbers, page numbers, house or room numbers, telephone numbers, serial numbers (for example, invoice, style, model, or lot numbers), and decimals.

1973   8760 Sunset Drive   846-0462

22. Some serial numbers (such as social security numbers) are written with hyphens, spaces, or other devices. Follow the style of the source.

Social Security No. 152-22-8285
License No. SO14 785 053

The Semicolon

1. When a coordinating conjunction (*and, but, or,* or *nor*) is omitted between two independent clauses, use a semicolon—not a comma—to separate the clauses.

The union was willing to compromise; the management was not.

a. Use a semicolon in order to achieve a stronger break between clauses than a comma provides.

Everyone is convinced that he could personally solve the problem if given the authority to do so; but no one will come forward with a clear-cut plan that we can evaluate in advance.

b. Use a semicolon when one or both clauses contain internal commas and a misreading might occur if a comma were also used to separate the clauses.

I sent you an order for bond letterheads, onionskin paper, carbons, and envelopes; and shipping tags, cardboard cartons, stapler wire, and binding tape were sent to me instead.

2. When independent clauses are linked by transitional expressions, use a semicolon between the clauses. (If the second

clause is long or requires special emphasis, treat it as a separate sentence.)

The motion was voted down; *moreover,* it was voted down by a large majority.

3. In general, when two independent clauses are linked by a transitional expression such as *for example* (abbreviated *e.g.*), *namely,* or *that is* (abbreviated *i.e.*), use a semicolon before the expression and a comma afterward.

He is highly qualified for the job; *for example,* he has had ten years' experience in the field.

4. Use a semicolon to separate items in a series if any of the items already contain commas.

Attending the conference in Washington were John Osgood, executive vice president; Donald Hays, marketing director; Charles Lindstrom, advertising manager; and Paul Hingle, sales promotion manager.

5. Use semicolons to separate a series of parallel subordinate clauses if they are long or contain internal commas. (However, a simple series of dependent clauses requires only commas, just like any other kind of series.)

He promised that he would review the existing specifications, costs, and sales estimates for the project; that he would analyze Merkle's alternative figures; and that he would prepare a detailed comparison of the two proposals.

The Colon

1. Use a colon between two independent clauses when the second clause explains or illustrates the first clause and there is no coordinating conjunction or transitional expression linking the two clauses.

The job you have described sounds very attractive: the salary is good and the opportunities for advancement seem excellent.

2. Place a colon before such expressions as *for example, namely,* and *that is* when they introduce words, phrases, or a series of clauses anticipated earlier in the sentence.

My assistant has three important duties: *namely,* attending all meetings, writing the minutes, and sending out notices.

3. When hours and minutes are expressed in figures, separate the figures by a colon, as in the expression 8:25. (No space precedes or follows this colon.)

4. A colon is used to represent the word *to* in proportions, as in the ratio 2:1. (No space precedes or follows this colon.)

5. In business letters, use a colon after the salutation. In social letters, use a comma.

The Dash

1. Use the dash to set off a parenthetical element that requires special emphasis.

We intend to see to it that our agents—as well as the transportation companies and the public—receive a fair decision in the matter.

2. Use a dash to show an abrupt break in thought or to set off an afterthought.

Here's gourmet food in a jiffy—economical too!

3. Use a dash to indicate hesitation, faltering speech, or stammering.

The work on the Lawson dam was begun—oh, I should say—well, about May 1—certainly no later than May 15.

4. Use dashes to set off single words that require special emphasis.

Money—that is all he thinks about.

5. Use dashes to set off and emphasize words that repeat or restate a previous thought.

Right now—at this very moment—our showrooms are crammed with bargains.

6. Use a dash before such words as *these, they,* and *all* when these words stand as subjects summarizing a preceding list of details.

A lawn mower, a rake, and a spade—these are the only tools you will need.

Parentheses

1. Use parentheses to enclose explanatory material that is independent of the main thought of the sentence.

We are disappointed at the very small number of people (five) who have accepted our invitation.

2. Use parentheses to set off references and directions.

Because of unusually heavy expenses to date (see the financial report attached), we are not in a position to make further changes this year.

3. Dates that accompany a person's name or an event are enclosed in parentheses.

Thomas Jefferson (1743–1826) was the third President of the United States.

4. Use parentheses to enclose numbers or letters that accompany enumerated items within a sentence.

We need the following information to complete our record of Mr. Rice's experience: (1) the number of years he worked for your company, (2) a description of his duties, and (3) the number of promotions he received.

5. Subdivisions in outlines are often enclosed in parentheses. When there are many gradations, it is sometimes necessary to use a single closing parenthesis to provide another grade.

```
1. Basic weaves I. . . . . . .
   a. Plain      A. . . . . . .
      (1) Basket    1. . . . . . .
      (2) Ribbed      a. . . . . . .
   b. Twill            (1) . . . . . .
      etc.               (a) . . . . . .
                            1) . . . . . .
                              a) . . . . . .
```

Quotation Marks

1. Use quotation marks to enclose a *direct quotation,* that is, the exact words of a speaker or a writer.

"I don't like the last paragraph in that letter," said Mr. Williams.

2. When only a word or phrase is quoted from another source, be sure to place the quotation marks around only the words extracted from the original source and not around any rearrangement of those words.

Bryant said he would decide when he had "all the facts." (Bryant's exact words were, "I will decide when I have all the facts.")

3. Words used humorously or ironically are enclosed in quotation marks.

They serve "fresh" vegetables all right—fresh out of the tin!

4. Slang or poor grammar that is purposely used is enclosed in quotation marks.

Whatever the true facts are, Jeff "ain't sayin'."

5. Words and phrases introduced by such expressions as *so-called, marked, signed,* and *entitled* are enclosed in quotation marks.

The carton was marked "Fragile."

6. Use quotation marks around titles that represent only *part* of a complete published work—for example, chapters, lessons, topics, sections, parts, tables, and charts within a book; articles and feature columns in newspapers and magazines; and essays, short poems, lectures, and sermons.

When you read Chapter 5, "The Effective Business Letter," give particular attention to the section headed "The Objectives of All Letter Writing."

7. Use quotation marks around the titles of *complete but unpublished* works, such as manuscripts, dissertations, and reports.

I would like to get a copy of Johnson's special study, "Criteria for Evaluating Staff Efficiency."

8. Use quotation marks around titles of songs and other short musical compositions, titles of paintings and pieces of sculpture, and titles of television and radio series and programs.

Everyone sang "Happy Birthday" to Mr. Parrott.

9. A quotation within another quotation is enclosed in single quotation marks. On a typewriter, use the apostrophe key for a single quotation mark.

"Suntanned skin became a fashionable 'must' about twenty or twenty-five years ago."

10. *Periods* and *commas* always go *inside* the closing quotation mark. (This placement is dictated solely on grounds of typographical appearance.)

Just as I was leaving his office, Mr. Brown called, "Miss Ward, I need five copies of that agreement."

The Underscore

1. A word referred to as a word is usually underscored, but it may be enclosed in quotation marks instead. A word referred to as a word is often introduced by the expression the term or the word.

The words carton and cartoon have quite different meanings. (ALSO: The words "carton" and "cartoon" have quite different meanings.)

2. In a formal definition the word to be defined is usually underscored and the definition is usually quoted. In this way the two elements may be easily distinguished.

the term psychosomatic has an interesting derivation: the prefix psycho means "of the mind"; the root word soma refers to the body.

3. Underscore foreign expressions that are not considered part of the English language. (Use quotation marks to set off translations of foreign expressions.)

A faux pas literally means "a false step."

4. Underscore titles of complete works that are published as separate items—for example, books, pamphlets, long poems, magazines, and newspapers. Also underscore titles of movies, plays, musicals, operas, and long musical compositions.

Every secretary will find <u>Etiquette in Business</u> helpful. (Titles of complete works may be typed in all capitals as an alternative to underscoring.)

The Apostrophe

1. The apostrophe is used to form the possessive of nouns and certain pronouns.

employee's record   one's choice

2. The apostrophe is used to indicate the omission of a letter or letters in a contraction.

doesn't   won't

3. The apostrophe may be used to form the plural of letters, figures, symbols, etc. However, the apostrophe is functionally unnecessary except where confusion might otherwise result.

PTA's or PTAs   1900's or 1900s
BUT: dotting the *i*'s

4. The apostrophe is used to indicate the omission of the first part of a date.

class of '70

5. The apostrophe is used as a single quotation mark.

Ellipsis Marks (...)

1. Ellipsis marks (three spaced periods with one typewriter space before and after each period) are often used, especially in advertising, to display individual items or to connect a series of loosely related phrases.

The Inn at the End of the Road . . . where you may enjoy the epicure's choicest offerings . . . by reservation only . . . closed Tuesdays.

2. Ellipsis marks are also used to indicate that a sentence trails off before the end.

He could easily have saved the situation by . . . But why talk about it.

The Asterisk (°)

The asterisk is used to refer the reader to a footnote, which usually is placed at the foot of a page.

"Because they won't let you wear it unless it fits." °

° Reg. U.S. Pat. Off.

The Diagonal (/)

1. The diagonal occurs (without space before or after) in certain abbreviations and symbols.

B/L   bill of lading   D/W   dock warrant
c/o   care of

2. The diagonal is also used in writing fractions (for example, 4/5) and in some code and serial numbers (for example, 2S/394756).

Brackets

A correction or an insertion in a quoted extract should be enclosed in brackets.

"During the height of the storm, winds exceeded 55 miles an hour [the local weather station recorded 60 miles an hour], with gusts up to 65 miles an hour."

Capitalization

1. Capitalize the first word of:
   a. Every sentence.

Up-to-date sales reports will be released tomorrow.

    b. An expression used as a sentence.

So much for that. Really? No!

    c. A quoted sentence.

Mr. Jarvis said, "The estimates will be submitted on Monday."

    d. An independent question within a sentence.

The question is, Will this policy reduce staff turnover?

    e. Each item displayed in a list or an outline.

    f. Each line in a poem. (Always follow the style of the poem itself, however.)

2. Capitalize every proper noun, that is, the official name of a particular person, place, or thing. Also capitalize adjectives derived from proper nouns.

George (n.), Georgian (adj.)
South America (n.), South American (adj.)

3. Capitalize imaginative names and nicknames that designate particular persons, places, or things.

the First Lady
the Windy City (for Chicago)

4. Capitalize a common noun when it is an actual part of a proper name. As a rule, however, do not capitalize the common-noun element when it is used alone in place of the full name.

Professor Burke   BUT: the professor
the Chase Corporation   the corporation

5. Capitalize all official titles of honor and respect when they *precede* personal names.

PROFESSIONAL TITLES:
Professor George Hamilton Booth   Dr. Morgan
CIVIC TITLES:
Governor Nelson Rockefeller
Ambassador Bunker

6. In general, do not capitalize titles of honor and respect when they *follow* a personal name or are used *in place of* a personal name.

Dr. Arthur Orwell, *president* of Cromwell University, will speak tomorrow night at eight. The *president's* topic is . . .

7. Capitalize words such as *mother, father, aunt, uncle,* etc., when they stand alone or are followed by a personal name.

I spoke to *Mother* and *Dad* on the phone last night.

8. Capitalize the names of companies, associations, societies, independent committees and boards, schools, political parties, conventions, fraternities, clubs, and religious bodies. (Follow the style established by the organization itself, as shown in the letterhead or some other written communication from the organization.)

the Anderson Hardware Company
the Young Women's Christian Association

9. Common organizational terms such as *advertising department, manufacturing division, finance committee,* and *board of directors* are ordinarily capitalized when they are the actual names of units within the writer's own organization. These terms are not capitalized when they refer to some other organization, unless the writer has reason to give these terms special importance or distinction.

The *Board of Directors* will meet next Thursday at 2:30. (From a company memorandum.)
BUT: Edward Perez has been elected to the *board of directors* of the Kensington Trade Corporation. (From a news release.)

10. Capitalize *the* preceding the name of an organization only when it is part of the legal name of the organization.

The Investment Company of America

11. Capitalize the names of countries and international organizations as well as national, state, county, and city bodies and their subdivisions.

the Republic of Panama   the Ohio Legislature

12. Capitalize short forms of names of national and international bodies and their major divisions.

the House (referring to the House of Representatives)

13. Capitalize *federal* only when it is part of the official name of a federal agency, a federal act, or some other proper noun.

the *Federal* Reserve Board
BUT: . . . Subject to federal, state, and local laws

14. Capitalize the names of places, such as streets, buildings, parks, monuments, rivers, oceans, and mountains. Do not capitalize short forms used in place of the full name.

Fulton Street   BUT: the street
the Empire State Building   the building

15. Capitalize the word *city* or *state* only when it is part of the corporate name of the city or state or part of an imaginative name.

Kansas City   BUT: the city of San Francisco
New York State is also called the Empire State.

16. Capitalize *north, south, east, west,* etc., when they designate definite regions or are an integral part of a proper name.

in the North   the Far North   North Dakota

17. Capitalize such words as *Northerner, Southerner,* and *Midwesterner.*

18. Capitalize *northern, southern, eastern, western,* etc., when these words pertain to the people in a region and to their political, social, or cultural activities. Do not capitalize these words, however, when they merely indicate general location or refer to the geography or climate of the region.

Eastern bankers   BUT: the eastern half of
                               Pennsylvania
Southern hospitality   southern
                               temperatures

19. Capitalize names of *days, months, holidays,* and *religious days.*

Wednesday   February

20. Capitalize the names of the seasons only when they are personified.

Come, gentle Spring.
BUT: Our order for *fall* merchandise was mailed today.

21. Capitalize the names of historical events and imaginative names given to historical periods.

the American Revolution   the Middle Ages

22. Do not capitalize the names of decades and centuries.

during the thirties   in the nineteen-seventies

23. Capitalize formal titles of acts, laws, bills, and treaties, but do not capitalize common-noun elements that stand alone in place of the full name.

the Social Security Act   BUT: the act

24. Capitalize the names of races, peoples, tribes, religions, and languages.

Chinese   Sanskrit

25. Do not capitalize the words *sun, moon,* or *earth* unless they are used in connection with the capitalized names of other planets or stars.

The *sun* was hidden behind a cloud.
In our astronomy class we have been comparing the orbits of Mars, Venus, and *Earth.*

26. Capitalize the names of specific courses of study. However, do not capitalize names of subjects or areas of study, except for any proper nouns or adjectives in such names.

American History 201 meets on Tuesdays and Thursdays. (Course title.)
Fred has decided to major in *American* history. (Area of study.)

27. Do not capitalize academic degrees used as general terms of classification (for example, a *bachelor of arts* degree). However, capitalize a degree used after a person's name (John Howard, *Doctor of Philosophy*).

28. Capitalize trademarks, brand names, proprietary names, names of commercial products, and market grades. The common

noun following the name of a product should not ordinarily be capitalized; however, manufacturers and advertisers often capitalize such words in the names of their own products for special emphasis.

Ivory soap   Hotpoint dishwasher

29. Capitalize all trade names except those that have become clearly established as common nouns. To be safe, check a dictionary, the *United States Government Printing Office Style Manual,* or (for the final authority) the trademark register in the U.S. Patent Office.

Coca-Cola, Coke   Teflon   BUT: nylon

30. Capitalize a noun followed by a number or a letter that indicates sequence. *Exceptions:* The nouns *line, note, page, paragraph, size,* and *verse* are not capitalized.

Act 1   Class 4   Lesson 20   Policy 394857

31. In titles of literary and artistic works and in displayed headings, capitalize all words with *four or more* letters. Also capitalize words with fewer than four letters except:
Articles: *the, a, an*
Short Conjunctions: *and, as, but, if, or, nor*
Short Prepositions: *at, by, for, in, of, off, on, out, to, up*

How to Succeed in Business Without Really Trying
"Redevelopment Proposal Is Not Expected to Be Approved"

Numbers

There are two basic number styles in wide use: the *figure style* (which uses figures for most numbers above 10) and the *word style* (which uses figures for most numbers above 100). The figure style is most commonly used in ordinary business correspondence. The word style is used in executive-level correspondence and in nontechnical material.

Figure Style

1. Spell out numbers from 1 through 10; use figures for numbers above 10. This rule applies to both exact and approximate numbers.

We ordered *ten* cases of yarn, but they can ship only *four* or *five*.
Please send us 35 copies of your latest bulletin.

Note: Even the numbers 1 through 10 may be expressed in figures (as in this sentence) when emphasis and quick comprehension are essential. This is the style used in tabulations and statistical matter, and in some offices it is the style used in sales letters and interoffice correspondence.

2. Use the same style to express *related* numbers above and below 10. (If most of the numbers are below 10, put them all in words; if most are above 10, express all in figures.)

Smoke damaged *five* dresses, *eight* suits, and *eleven* coats.

3. For fast comprehension, numbers in the *millions* or higher may be expressed as follows:

21 million (in place of 21,000,000)
14½ million (in place of 14,500,000)

    a. This style may be used only when the amount consists of a whole number with nothing more than a simple fraction or decimal following. A number such as 4,832,067 must be written all in figures.

b. Treat related numbers alike.

Last year we sold 21,557,000 items; this year, nearly 23,000,000. (NOT: 23 million)

Word Style

1. Spell out all numbers, whether exact or approximate, that can be expressed in one or two words. (A hyphenated compound number like *twenty-one* or *ninety-nine* counts as one word.) In effect, spell out all numbers from 1 through 100 and all round numbers above 100 that require no more than two words (such as *sixty-two thousand* or *forty-five million*).

Mr. Ryan received *twenty-three* letters praising his talk at the Rotary Club.

2. Express related numbers the same way, even though some are above 100 and some below.

We sent out *three hundred* invitations and have already received over *one hundred* acceptances.

3. When spelling out large round numbers, use the shortest form possible.

We have distributed over *twelve hundred* copies of our prospectus.

4. Numbers in the millions or higher *that require more than two words when spelled out* may be expressed as follows:

231 million (in place of 231,000,000)
9¼ billion (in place of 9,250,000,000)

5. Always spell out a number that begins a sentence.

Forty-six glasses were broken.

6. For consistency, also spell out related numbers.

Twenty to *thirty* percent of the goods received were defective. (NOT: Twenty to 30 percent.)

7. If the numbers are large (requiring more than two words when spelled out) or if figures are preferable (for emphasis or quick reference), rearrange the wording of the sentence.

The company sent out 298 circulars. (INSTEAD of: *Two hundred and ninety-eight* circulars were sent out by the company.)

8. Always spell out indefinite numbers and amounts.

a few hundred votes   hundreds of customers

Ordinals

1. Spell out all ordinals (*first*, *second*, *third*, etc.) that can be expressed in one or two words.

2. Figures are used to express ordinals in certain expressions of dates, in numbered street names above 10, and occasionally in displayed headings and titles for special effect.
Note: Ordinal figures are expressed as follows: *1st, 2d or 2nd, 3d or 3rd, 4th, 5th, 6th,* etc. Do not use an "abbreviation period" following an ordinal.

Dates

1. When the day *precedes* the month or *stands* alone, express it either in ordinal figures (*1st, 2d, 3d, 4th,* etc.) or in ordinal words (the *first,* the *twelfth,* the *twenty-eighth*).

Our meeting starts on the *25th* of July and continues until the *29th*. (Figure style.)

2. When the day *follows* the month, always express it in cardinal figures (*1, 2, 3,* etc.).

on March 6 (NOT: March 6th or March sixth)

3. Express complete dates in month-day-year sequence.

March 6, 1969

4. In United States military correspondence and in letters from foreign countries, the complete date is expressed in day-month-year sequence.

15 September 1969

5. In legal documents, proclamations, and formal invitations, spell out the day and the year. A number of styles may be used.

May twenty-first   nineteen hundred and sixty-nine

6. Class graduation years and well-known years in history may appear in abbreviated form.

the class of '74

Money

1. Use figures to express exact or approximate amounts of money.

$5   about $200

2. Spell out indefinite amounts of money; for example, *a few million dollars, many thousands of dollars.*

3. Do not add a decimal point or ciphers to a whole dollar amount when it occurs in a sentence.

I am enclosing a check for *$125* as payment in full.

In tabulations, however, if any amount in the column contains cents, add a decimal point and two ciphers to all *whole* dollar amounts to maintain a uniform appearance.

$150.50
  25.00
   8.05
———
$183.55

4. Money in round amounts of a million or more may be expressed partially in words.

$12 million	OR	12 million dollars
$10½ million	OR	10½ million dollars

    a. This style may be used only when the amount consists of a whole number with nothing more than a simple fraction or decimal following. An amount like *$10,235,000* must be written entirely in figures.

    b. Express related amounts the same way.

from $500,000 to $1,000,000
(NOT: from $500,000 to $1 million)

    c. Repeat the word *million* (*billion,* etc.) with each figure to avoid misunderstanding.

$5 million to $10 million
NOT: $5 to $10 million)

5. Fractional expressions of large amounts of money should be either completely spelled out or converted to an all-figure style.

one-quarter of a million dollars OR $250,000
(BUT NOT: ¼ of a million dollars OR $¼ million)

6. For amounts under a dollar, use figures and the word *cents*.

I am sure that customers will not pay more than *50 cents* for this item.

Note: An isolated, nonemphatic reference to cents may be spelled out.

I wouldn't give *two cents* for that car.

    a. Do not use the style *$.75* in sentences except when related amounts require a dollar sign.

Prices for the principal grains were as follows: wheat, $1.73; corn, $1.23; oats, $.78; rye, $1.58.

    b. The symbol ¢ should be used only in technical and statistical matter containing many price quotations.

Yesterday's wholesale prices for food commodities were as follows: coffee, 42¢; cocoa, 23¢; sugar, 7¢; butter, 66¢.

7. When using the dollar sign or the cent sign with a price range or a series of amounts, use the sign with each amount.

$5,000 to $10,000   10¢ to 20¢

If the term *dollars* or *cents* is to be spelled out, use it only with the final amount.

10 to 20 cents

Measurements

1. Most measurements have a technical significance and should be expressed in figures for emphasis or quick comprehension. However, spell out a measurement that lacks technical significance.

A higher rate is charged on parcels over 2 *pounds*.
BUT: I'm afraid I've gained another *two pounds* this week.

Note: Dimensions, sizes, and temperature readings are always expressed in figures.

The dimensions of his office are 12 by 14 feet.

2. When a measurement consists of several words, do not use commas to separate the words. The measurement is considered a single unit. The unit of measure may be abbreviated or expressed as a symbol only in technical matter or tabular work.

The parcel weighed 6 *pounds 14 ounces*.
I am 6 *feet 2 inches* tall.

Fractions

1. A mixed number (a whole number plus a fraction) is written in figures except at the beginning of a sentence.

This year's sales are $3\frac{1}{4}$ times as great as they were five years ago.

2. A fraction that stands alone (without a whole number preceding) should be expressed in words unless the spelled-out form is long and awkward or unless the fraction is used in technical writing.

one-half the vote   three-fourths of the voters

3. Fractions expressed in figures should not be followed by *st, ds, nds,* or *ths* or by an *of* phrase.

3/200 (NOT: 3/200ths)

If a sentence requires the use of an *of* phrase following the fraction, spell the fraction out.

three-quarters of an hour (NOT: ¾ of an hour)

Decimals

1. Always write decimals in figures. Never insert commas in the decimal part of a number.

665.3184368 (no comma in decimal part of the number)

2. When a decimal stands alone (without a whole number preceding the decimal point), insert a cipher before the decimal point unless the decimal itself begins with a cipher. (Reason: The cipher prevents the reader from overlooking the decimal point.)

0.55 inch   .06 gram

3. Do not begin a sentence with a decimal figure.

The temperature reading at 8 a.m. was 63.7.
(NOT: 63.7 was the temperature reading at 8 a.m.)

Percentages

1. Express percentages in figures, and spell out the word *percent.*

He is willing to give us a discount of *15 percent.*

Note: The % symbol is used only in tabulations, business forms, interoffice memorandums, and statistical or technical matter.

2. Fractional percentages *under 1 percent* should be spelled out or expressed as a decimal figure.

one-half of 1 percent OR 0.5 percent

3. In a range or series of percentages, the word *percent* follows the last figure only. The symbol %, if used, must follow each figure.

Price reductions range from *20 to 50 percent.*
BUT: from 20% to 50%

Ratios and Proportions

Always write ratios and proportions in figures.

a 5 to 1 ratio   OR   a 5:1 ratio

Ages and Anniversaries

1. In general, spell out numbers designating ages and anniversaries.

Mary is *nineteen* years old.
Sam is *sixty-eight* years of age.

2. Use figures to express ages and anniversaries if they are used as technical measurements or as significant statistics (as in news releases, personal data sheets, and matters pertaining to employment, retirement, insurance, and the like). Also use figures when the number would require more than two words if spelled out.

Ralph Thompson, *40*, has been promoted to professor of law.
The Hamden Corporation will be celebrating its *125th* anniversary next month.

3. Use figures for ages expressed in years, months, and days. Do not use commas to separate the elements; they are considered to make up a single unit.

On June 13 he will be 19 years 4 months and 17 days old. (The *and* linking months and days is often omitted.)

Periods of Time

1. In general, express periods of time in words.

a twenty-minute wait   in twenty-four months

2. Use figures to express periods of time when they are used as technical measurements or significant statistics (as in discounts, interest rates, and credit terms). Also use figures when the number would require more than two words if spelled out.

a 5-minute warmup   a note due in 6 months   350 years ago

Clock Time

1. Always use figures with *a.m.* or *p.m.*

The boat sails at 11:30 *a.m.*

a. The abbreviations *a.m.* and *p.m.* are typed in small letters without spaces. (In printed matter they usually appear in small capitals.)

b. When expressing time "on the hour," do not add ciphers to denote minutes except in tables where other times are given in hours and minutes.

Our store is open from 9:30 a.m. to 6 *p.m.*

c. Do not use *a.m.* or *p.m.* unless figures are used.

this morning (NOT: this a.m.)

    d. Do not use *a.m.* or *p.m.* with *o'clock*

6 o'clock   OR   6 p.m.
(NOT: 6 p.m. o'clock)

    e. Do not use *a.m.* or *p.m.* with the expressions *in the morning, in the afternoon, in the evening,* or *at night.* The abbreviations themselves already convey one of these meanings.

at 9 p.m.   OR   at nine in the evening
(NOT: at 9 p.m. in the evening)

    f. The times *noon* and *midnight* may be expressed in words alone. However, use the forms *12 noon* and *12 midnight* when these times are given with other times expressed in figures.

The second shift ends at *midnight.*
BUT: The second shift runs from *4 p.m.* to *12 midnight.*

    2. With *o'clock* use figures for emphasis or words for formality.

3 o'clock (figure style)
three o'clock (word style)

    3. When expressing time "on the hour" without *a.m., p.m.,* or *o'clock,* spell the hour out.

He will arrive at *eight* tonight. (NOT: at 8 tonight.)

Scores and Voting Results

    Use figures (even for 1 through 10) to express scores and voting results.

a score of 85 on the test   a vote of 17 to 6

Serial Numbers

Always use figures to express serial numbers (invoice, style, model, lot numbers, etc.), telephone numbers, house or room numbers, page numbers, and the like. Do not use commas to set off "thousands" in such numbers.

(516) 783-9097   Column 6   page 1112

With Abbreviations and Symbols

Always use figures with abbreviations and symbols.

$25   90¢   50%

Numbers in a Sequence

1. Use commas to separate numbers that do not represent a continuous sequence.

on pages 18, 20, and 28
data for the years 1945, 1950, and 1955

2. A hyphen may be used in place of the word *to* to link two figures that represent a continuous sequence.

on pages 18-28   in Articles 1-111

No. or # With Figures

1. If the term *number* precedes a figure, express it as an abbreviation (singular: *No.*; plural, *Nos.*). At the beginning of a sentence, however, spell out *Number* to prevent misreading.

Our check covers the following invoices: Nos. 592, 653, and 654.
Number 82175 has been assigned to your new policy.

2. The symbol # may be used on business forms (such as invoices) and in technical matter.

Word Division

1. Words may be divided only between syllables. Whenever you are unsure of the syllabication of a word, consult a dictionary.

2. Do not divide one-syllable words. Even when *ed* is added to some words, they still remain one-syllable words and cannot be divided.

weight   passed

3. Do not set off a one-letter syllable at the beginning or the end of a word.

amount (NOT: a- mount)   ideal (NOT: i- deal)

4. Do not divide a word unless you can leave a syllable of at least three characters (the last of which is the hyphen) on the upper line and you can carry a syllable of at least three characters (the last may be a punctuation mark) to the next line.

ad- joining   *un*- important
bluff- *ing*   check- *up,*

5. Do not divide abbreviations.

ILGWU   Ph.D.

Note: An abbreviation such as *AFL-CIO* could be divided after the hyphen.

6. Do not divide contractions.

doesn't   couldn't

7. Divide a solid compound word between the elements of the compound.

business- man   time- table
home- owner   sales- woman

8. Divide a hyphenated compound word at the point of the hyphen.

self- control   brother- in-law
get- together   baby- sitter

9. Divide a word *after* a prefix (rather than within the prefix).

Preferred   *Acceptable*
. . . . . .intro-   . . . . . .in-
duce . . . . . .   troduce . . .

10. Divide a word *before* a suffix (rather than within the suffix).

practi- cable (RATHER THAN: practica- ble

11. When a word has both a prefix and a suffix, choose the division point that groups the syllables more intelligibly.

consign- ment (RATHER THAN: con- signment)

12. Whenever you have a choice, divide after a prefix or before a suffix (rather than within the root word).

pre-mature (RATHER THAN: prema- ture)

13. When a one-letter syllable occurs within the root of a word, divide *after* it (rather than before it).

criti- cal   sepa- rate

14. When two separately sounded vowels come together in a word, divide between them (rather than immediately before or after them).

radi- ator   gradu- ation

15. Try to keep together certain kinds of word groups that need to be read together—for example, page and number, month and day, month and year, title and surname, surname and abbreviation, number and abbreviation, or number and unit of measure.

page 63   January 16

16. When necessary, longer word groups may be divided according to the following rules:

    a. Dates may be divided between the day and year.

. . . . .September 21,   NOT:. . . . . .September
1971 . . . .   21, 1971 . . . . . .

    b. *Street addresses* may be divided between the name of
       the street and *Street, Avenue,* etc.

. . . . . .914 Glen   NOT: 914
Avenue . . . . . .   Glen Avenue . . .

    c. *Names of places* may be divided between the city and
       the state.

. . . . . .Cincinnati,
Ohio . . . .

    d. *Names of persons* may be divided between the given
       name (including middle initial if given) and surname.

. . . . . .William E.   NOT:. . . . . William
Roberts . . . . . .   E. Roberts. . . . . . .

> e. *Names preceded by very long titles* may be divided be-
> tween the title and the name.

. . . . . .The Reverend
Henry S. Brewster . . .

> f. A *numbered or lettered list* may be divided before any
> number or letter.

. . . . . . .these points:
(1) All cards should . . .
NOT: . . . . . . .these points: (1)
     All cards should . . . . .

17. Do not allow more than two consecutive lines to end in
hyphens.

18. Do not divide at the end of the first line or the last full
line in a paragraph.

19. Do not divide the last word on a page.

Abbreviations

1. Use abbreviations and contractions sparingly.

2. Be consistent within the same letter, report, or manuscript.
Do not abbreviate a term in some sentences and spell it out in
other sentences.

3. When you do abbreviate, use the generally accepted forms.
A number of abbreviations have alternative forms, with differences in spelling, capitalization, and punctuation. Again, be

consistent: having selected one particular style for an abbreviation (say, *a.m.*), do not use a different style (*A.M.*) elsewhere in the same material.

4. In sentences, when only the surname is used, spell out all titles except *Mr., Mrs., Messrs.,* and *Dr.*

Mr. Ames will be the guest of *Professor* and *Mrs.* King.

Note: In formal writing, *Dr.* may be spelled out when used with only the surname.

5. Abbreviations of academic degrees require a period after each element in the abbreviation but no internal space.

B.A.   Ph.D.   LL.B.

6. Names of well-known business organizations, labor unions, societies, and associations (trade, professional, charitable, and fraternal) often appear in abbreviated form, except in the most formal writing. When these abbreviations consist of all-capital initials, they are typed without periods or spaces.

IBM   AT&T   AFL-CIO

7. The names of radio and television broadcasting stations and the abbreviated names of broadcasting systems are written in capitals without periods and without spaces.

Station KFRC   CBS officials

8. The name United States is often abbreviated when it is part of the name of a government agency. In all other uses, however, it should be spelled out.

U.S. Office of Education OR USOE

9. Geographical abbreviations made up of single initials require a period after each initial but *no* space after each internal period. If the geographical abbreviation contains more than single initials, space once after each internal period.

U.S.A.   U.S.S.R.   N. Mex.   N. Dak.

10. Do not abbreviate names of days of the week and months of the year except in tables or lists where space is limited. In such cases the following abbreviations may be used.

Sun.	Jan.	July, Jul.
Mon.	Feb.	Aug.
Tues., Tue.	Mar.	Sept., Sep.
Wed.	Apr.	Oct.
Thurs., Thu.	May	Nov.
Fri.	June, Jun.	Dec.
Sat.		

11. Use the abbreviations *a.m.* and *p.m.* in expressions of time. Small letters are preferred for these abbreviations.

12. A few common business abbreviations are often typed in small letters (with periods) when they occur within sentences, but are typed in all-capital letters (without periods) when they appear on invoices or other business forms.

c.o.d.	OR COD	cash on delivery
f.o.b.	OR FOB	free on board

13. Do not use periods with capitalized letters that are not abbreviations.

IOU   SOS   Brand X

14. The abbreviation OK is now commonly written without periods. In sentences, the forms *okay, okayed,* and *okaying* look better than *OK, OK'd,* and *OK'ing,* but the latter forms can be used.

15. Small-letter abbreviations made up of single initials require a period after each initial but no space after each internal period.

a.m.   p.m.   f.o.b.

16. All-capital abbreviations made up of single initials normally require *no periods* and *no internal space*.

RCA   FBI   IQ

17. If an abbreviation contains more than single initials, space once after each internal period.

sq. ft.   op. cit.

18. Initials in a person's name (or in a company name) should each be followed by a period and one space.

John T. Noonan   L. B. Anders, Inc.

19. *One* space should follow an abbreviation within a sentence unless another mark of punctuation must follow immediately.

Please call tomorrow afternoon (before 5:30 p.m.).

20. *Two* spaces should follow an abbreviation at the end of a statement.

The vase dates back to 400 B.C. The picture is more recent.

21. *No* space should follow an abbreviation at the end of a question or an exclamation.

Can you see me tomorrow at 10:30 a.m.?

Letters and Memos

Letterhead or Return Address

1. Ordinarily business letters are written on stationery with a printed letterhead containing at least these elements: company name; street address; city, state, and ZIP Code; area code and telephone number. When using plain paper instead of printed letterhead stationery, include a return address on the first page of the letter.

    a. If you use a *return address,* type the street address on the thirteenth line from the top of the page and the city, state, and ZIP Code on the fourteenth line. Except in the full-blocked and simplified letter arrangements (see Letter Styles 3 and 6 on pages 238 and 241), start each line of the return address at the center of the page or position the longest line so that it ends at the right margin (as shown below).

2550 Mulberry Street
New York, New York 10012

Date Line

1. In business correspondence:

    a. The date line consists of the *name of the month,* written in full—never abbreviated or represented by figures; the *day,* written in figures and followed by a comma; and the *complete year;* for example, *December 8, 1972.* Never use the styles *12/8/72, 2/8/72,* or *'72* because the dates they represent are easily confused.

    b. When using letterhead stationery, position the date on the fifteenth line from the top of the page or three lines below the letterhead, whichever is lower. The date line usually begins at the center of the page or ends at the right margin; however, it may be positioned in some other attractive relationship to the letterhead design. In the full-blocked and simplified arrangements (see Letter Styles 3 and 6), the date line begins at the left margin.

c. When using a return address, type the date on the line below the city and state and begin it at the same point as the other lines in the return address.

2. In military correspondence:

a. The date line usually consists of the day, the month, and the year, in that order; for example, *15 June 1972.*

3. In correspondence from some foreign countries, the date may be written with the month between the day and the year; for example, *10 August 1972.*

Personal or Confidential Notation

If a letter is of a personal or confidential nature, type the word *Personal* or *Confidential* in all-capital letters and underscore it. Position this notation on the second line below the date, at the *left* margin.

Inside Address

a. The inside address of a business letter must contain at least the following information: (1) the name of the person or the company to whom you are writing, or both; (2) the street address; (3) the city, state, and ZIP Code (see Letter Styles 2 and 3). It may include such additional information as the person's job title and his department (see Letter Style 4).

b. The inside address should begin on the third line below the personal or confidential notation, if used, or on the fifth line below the date.

c. The inside address should be single-spaced.

See Letter Styles 1 to 6, pages 236–241, for the arrangement of inside addresses.

Name of Person and Title

1. When writing the name of a person in an inside address or elsewhere be sure to follow the spelling and capitalization that the owner of the name uses. In order to verify the correctness of a name, you may need to consult original correspondence from that person, a mailing list, a directory, or the person who dictated the letter you are typing.

a. Note the differences in spelling, capitalization, and spacing in names containing the prefixes *Mac* and *Mc*.

Macmillan, MacMillan, Mac Millan, Macmillen, MacMillen, McMillan, Mc Millan, McMillen, McMillin

b. In names containing the prefix *O'*, always capitalize the *O* and the letter following the apostrophe; for example, *O'Brian* or *O'Brien*.

c. Watch for differences in spacing and capitalization in names containing the prefixes *d', da, de, del, della, di, du, la, le, van, von,* etc.

D'Amato, Damato
D'Amelio, d'Amelio
van Auken, Van Auken, VanAuken

de laFuente, DeLaFuente,
De laFuente

Note: When a surname with an uncapitalized prefix stands alone (that is, without a first name, a title, or initials preceding it), capitalize the prefix to prevent misreading.

George de Luca   Mr. de Luca   G. R. de Luca
BUT: I hear that De Luca is leaving the company.

d. Do not abbreviate or use initials unless the person to whom you are writing uses an abbreviation or initials; for example, do not write *Mr. Wm. B. Sachs* or *Mr. W. B. Sachs* if the person to whom you are writing used *William B. Sachs.* *Note:* When names that contain prefixes and particles are to be typed in all-capital letters, follow these principles: If there is no space after the prefix, capitalize only the initial letter of the prefix. If space follows the prefix, capitalize the entire prefix.

NORMAL FORM   ALL-CAPITAL FORM
MacDonald   MacDONALD
But: Mac Donald MAC DONALD

2. In an inside address, always use a title before the name of a person unless the abbreviation of an academic degree, such as *M.D.* or *Ph.D.*, or the abbreviation *Esq.* (which stands for *Esquire* and which is sometimes used after the name of a lawyer) is to appear after the name.

a. If the person has no special title, such as *Dr., Professor,* or *Honorable,* use the courtesy title *Mr., Mrs.,* or *Miss.* Use *Master* before the name of a young boy.

b. If there is no way to determine whether the person is a man or a woman, use the title *Mr.*

c. If there is no way to determine the marital status of a woman, use the title *Miss.* (The abbreviation *Ms.,* meaning "Miss" or "Mrs.," is also acceptable in ambiguous situations.)

d. If a letter is intended for two or more men, use the title *Messrs.* (plural of *Mr.*); for two or more married women, use *Mesdames* (plural of *Mrs.*); for two or more unmarried women, use *Misses* (plural of *Miss*).

e. Long titles, such as *Lieutenant, Governor,* and *Superintendent,* should be spelled out in formal correspondence. They may be abbreviated in informal correspondence.

f. *The Reverend* and *The Honorable* are titles of respect, not of rank or office. They should be spelled out in formal correspondence, but they may be abbreviated in informal correspondence; for example, *Rev. James Lee, Hon. Shirley Chisholm.*

g. If a letter is being addressed to more than one person, be sure to use the appropriate title with each name when a plural title, such as *Messrs.* or *Professors,* does not apply to all the persons.

Dr. and Mrs. Herbert Booth

If a letter is being addressed to two persons with different surnames, type each name on a separate line.

Dr. Paul J. Rogers
Mr. James A. Davis

3. When *Jr., Sr.,* or a roman numeral such as *III* is typed after a name, use a comma before *Jr.* or *Sr.* but not before a roman numeral. (Even the comma before *Jr.* and *Sr.* is increasingly being dropped.)

4. Abbreviations of academic degrees, such as *M.D.,* and of religious orders, such as *S.J.,* are typed after names and preceded by a comma.

5. A title of position, such as *Vice President* or *Vocational Director*, should be included in an inside address when possible. If the title is short, it may be typed on the same line as the person's name and preceded by a comma. If the title is long, type it on the line following the name; if the title runs on to a second line, indent the turnover two spaces.

Mr. J. C. Lee, President   Mrs. Helen Hansen
                                  Executive Vice President
Mr. Ralph Nielsen
Vice President and
   General Manager

Note: Capitalize a title that accompanies a name in an address.

6. Never use two titles that mean the same thing with a name; for example, *Dr. George M. Wharton, Ph.D.*, would be incorrect. Address the letter to *Dr. George M. Wharton* or to *George M. Wharton, Ph.D.*

Name of Firm

1. When writing the name of a firm in an inside address or elsewhere, always use the official name and follow the company's style for spelling, punctuation, capitalization, spacing, and abbreviations. The letterhead of incoming correspondence is the best source for this information. Note the variations in style in these names:

Time Inc.
Thyme Inc.
Faber & Faber, Ltd.
Abelard-Schuman, Limited
Mekler / Ansell Associates Inc.
Post-Keyes-Gardner Inc.
Merrill Lynch, Pierce, Fenner & Smith Inc.
Webster Sheffield Fleischmann Hitchcock & Brookfield

2. If the official form cannot be ascertained from incoming correspondence, follow these general rules:

a. Use the ampersand (&) rather than *and* when the company name consists of the names of persons.

Curtis & Hall, Inc.   BUT: Acme Lead and Tin Company

b. Write *Inc.* for *Incorporated* and *Ltd.* for *Limited,* and precede the abbreviation by a comma.

c. As a rule, spell out *Company* or *Corporation;* if the name is extremely long, however, use the abbreviation *Co.* or *Corp.*

d. Do not capitalize the word *the* at the beginning of a name unless you are sure it is part of the official name; for example, *The Rand Corporation.*

e. Use an apostrophe if the name includes a singular possessive noun or an irregular plural noun; for example, *Harper's Bazaar, The Children's Shop.* Do not use an apostrophe if the name includes a regular plural noun; for example, *American Bankers Association.*

3. Ordinarily, type the firm name on a line by itself.

Building Name

If the name of a building is included in the inside address, type it on a line by itself immediately above the street address.

Street Address

1. Always type the street address on a line by itself.

2. Use figures for house, building, apartment, room, or rural route numbers. Do not include the abbreviation *No.* or the symbol # before such numbers.
EXCEPTION: For clarity, the word *One* instead of the figure *1* is generally used in a house or building number; for example, *One Park Avenue.*

3. Numbers used as street names are written as follows:

a. Spell out the numbers 1 through 10; for example, *177 Second Avenue.*

b. Use figures for numbers over 10; for example, *27 East 22d Street* or *27 East 22 Street.* The ordinal sign *st, d,* or *th* may be omitted so long as a word such as *East* or *West* separates the street number from the building number. If no such word intervenes, use the ordinal sign for clarity; for example, *144 65th Street.*

4. Do not abbreviate *North, South, East, West, Northeast, Southwest,* or a similar word when it appears before the street name; for example, *330 West 42 Street.*

5. Type an abbreviation representing a section of a city after the street name and use a comma before it; for example, *2012 Massachusetts Avenue, N.W.*

6. Use the word *and,* not an ampersand (&), in a street address; for example, *Tenth and Market Streets.*

7. Avoid abbreviating such words as *Street* and *Avenue* whenever possible.

City, State, and Zip Code

1. The city, state, and ZIP Code must always be typed on one line, immediately following the street address. Type the name of the city, followed by a comma and one space; the state, followed by one space but no comma; and the ZIP Code. (See Letter Styles 2, 3, 4, and 5.)

2. When writing the name of a city in an address:

a. Never use an abbreviation (for example, *Chic.* for Chicago).

b. Never abbreviate the words *Fort, Mount, Point,* or *Port.* Write the name of the city in full. For example: *Fort Dodge, Mount Vernon, Point Pleasant, Port Huron.*

c. Abbreviate the word *Saint* in the names of American cities; for example, *St. Louis, St. Paul.*

3. In an address, the name of the state may be spelled out or abbreviated as follows:

	New	*Old*		*New*	*Old*
Alabama	AL	Ala.	Missouri	MO	Mo.
Alaska	AK	. . .	Montana	MT	Mont.
Arizona	AZ	Ariz.	Nebraska	NB	Nebr.
Arkansas	AR	Ark.	Nevada	NV	Nev.
California	CA	Calif.	New Hampshire	NH	N.H.
Canal Zone	CZ	C.Z.	New Jersey	NJ	N.J.
Colorado	CO	Colo.	New Mexico	NM	N. Mex.
Connecticut	CT	Conn.	New York	NY	N.Y.
Delaware	DE	Del.	North Carolina	NC	N.C.
District			North Dakota	ND	N. Dak.
of Columbia	DC	D.C.	Ohio	OH	. . .
Florida	FL	Fla.	Oklahoma	OK	Okla.
Georgia	GA	Ga.	Oregon	OR	Oreg.
Guam	GU	. . .	Pennsylvania	PA	Pa.
Hawaii	HI	. . .	Puerto Rico	PR	P.R.
Idaho	ID	. . .	Rhode Island	RI	R.I.
Illinois	IL	Ill.	South Carolina	SC	S.C.
Indiana	IN	Ind.	South Dakota	SD	S. Dak.
Iowa	IA	. . .	Tennessee	TN	Tenn.
Kansas	KS	Kans.	Texas	TX	Tex.
Kentucky	KY	Ky.	Utah	UT	. . .
Louisiana	LA	La.	Vermont	VT	Vt.
Maine	ME	. . .	Virgin Islands	VI	V.I.
Maryland	MD	Md.	Virginia	VA	Va.
Massachusetts	MA	Mass.	Washington	WA	Wash.
Michigan	MI	Mich.	West Virginia	WV	W. Va.
Minnesota	MN	Minn.	Wisconsin	WI	Wis.
Mississippi	MS	Miss.	Wyoming	WY	Wyo.

a. Though they may be used in other situations, the new two-letter state abbreviations were created by the U.S. Post

Office Department specifically for use in address blocks on envelopes. However, for the sake of consistency, the style used in the envelope address should be used in the inside address of a letter.

b. Writers who regard the two-letter abbreviations as too informal to be used on all correspondence may elect to spell out state names in most cases and to use the abbreviations only in informal correspondence.

c. Always type the two-letter state abbreviations in capital letters, with no periods after or space between the letters.

d. When an address is written in a sentence, spell out the name of the state; leave one space between the state and the ZIP Code.

My address next month will be 501 South 71 Court, Miami, Florida 33144, but mail sent to my office will reach me just as easily.

4. Do not include the name of a county or an area (such as *Long Island*) in an address.

5. In a Canadian address, spell out or abbreviate the name of the province as follows:

Alberta	Alta.
British Columbia	B.C.
Manitoba	Man.
New Brunswick	N.B.
Newfoundland	Nfld.
Nova Scotia	N.S.
Ontario	Ont.
Prince Edward Island	P.E.I.
Quebec	Que. OR P.Q.
Saskatchewan	Sask.

6. In a foreign address, type the name of the country on a separate line in all-capital letters. Do not abbreviate the name of the country. EXCEPTION: U.S.S.R. (Union of Soviet Socialist Republics).

Mr. Ralph P. Williams
Robinson & Young, Ltd.
50 York Street
Toronto 1, Ontario
CANADA

Mr. H. Andrew Koyama
1-504 Kitaisogo-Danchi
Isogo-Ku
Yokohama
JAPAN

Attention Line

When a letter is addressed to a company, an attention line may be used to direct the letter to a particular person or department. The attention line should be typed on the second line below the inside address. It may start at the left margin, it may be indented the same as the paragraphs, or it may be centered. It may be typed in all-capital letters, or it may be typed in capital and small letters, with the complete line or only the word *Attention* underscored. The word *Attention* should not be abbreviated; it need not be followed by the word *of* or a colon. (See also Letter Style 2.) Two common typewritten styles are as follows:

ATTENTION SALES MANAGER   Attention Mr. Ellery

Salutation

1. Type the salutation, beginning at the left margin, on the second line below the attention line (if used) or on the second line below the inside address. Follow the salutation with a colon unless you are using open punctuation (see Letter Style 3).

2. Abbreviate only the titles *Mr., Mrs., Messrs.,* and *Dr.* (In formal correspondence, the title *Doctor* may be spelled out.) All other titles, such as *Professor* and *Father,* should always be written out. (See Forms of Address section for military titles.)

3. Capitalize the first word as well as any nouns and titles in the salutation; for example, *Dear Sir, My dear Mr. Brand, Right Reverend and dear Sir.*

4. The following are approved forms of salutation:

To one person
Customary: Dear Mr. Smith: Dear Miss Simpson:
More formal: My dear Mr. Smith:
                                    My dear Miss Simpson:
Formal and impersonal: Dear Sir: Dear Madam:
Very formal (official):   Sir: Madam:

CAUTION: Never write just *Dear Miss;* always include a surname.

To two men
Customary: Dear Mr. Brown and Mr. Jones:
                                    OR: Gentlemen:
More formal: My dear Messrs. Brown and Jones:
  To two women
Customary—Married: Dear Mrs. Brown and Mrs. Jones:
          Unmarried: Dear Miss Allen and Miss Davis:
More formal—Married: My dear Mesdames Brown and Jones:
            Unmarried: My dear Misses Allen and Davis:
To a man and a woman: Dear Miss Allen and Mr. Kent:
To an organization: Gentlemen:
To an organization   Mesdames: OR Ladies:
  composed entirely
  of women:

Note: When an attention line is used, the salutation must always be *Gentlemen* (or, if appropriate, *Mesdames* or *Ladies*). Reason: The letter is addressed to an organization, not to one person.

Subject Line

a. Type the subject line (if given) on the second line below the salutation. You may start it at the left margin, indent it the same as the paragraphs, or center it. Type it either in all-

capital letters or in capital and small letters that are underscored.

MORAN LEASE   *Introductory Offer to New Subscribers*

b. The term *Subject:* or (in legal correspondence) *In re:* often
precedes the actual subject. (See also Letter Style 3.)

SUBJECT: MORAN LEASE   *In re: Moran Lease*

Body of Letter

1. Begin the body of the letter on the second line below the
subject line, if used, or on the second line below the salutation.
EXCEPTION: In the simplified letter (see Letter Style 6), the
body starts on the third line.

2. In the semiblocked letter style (see Letter Style 2), indent
the first line of each paragraph. (Although five spaces is the
usual indention, some writers prefer to indent up to ten spaces.)

3. Use single spacing and leave one blank line between paragraphs.

Complimentary Closing

1. Type the complimentary closing on the second line below
the last line of the body of the letter. If the full-blocked or
square-blocked letter style is used, start the closing at the left
margin (see Letter Styles 3 and 4). Otherwise, start the closing
at the center or at the point at which the date line begins.

2. Capitalize only the first word of a complimentary closing.
Place a comma at the end of the line (except when open punctuation is used).

3. If the dictator does not dictate the complimentary closing,
use one of these:

a. Personal in tone: *Sincerely, Cordially, Sincerely yours, Cordially yours.*

b. More formal in tone: *Yours truly, Yours very truly, Very truly yours, Very sincerely yours, Very cordially yours.*

c. If an informal closing phrase, such as *Best wishes* or *Kindest regards,* is used instead of a regular complimentary closing, type the phrase in the complimentary-closing position and follow it by a comma.

Note: Once a pattern of informal phrases is begun with a customer, it should not be discontinued without good reason. Otherwise, if a closing returns to a more formal phrasing, the customer will wonder what has happened.

Company Signature

1. A company signature may be used to emphasize the fact that a letter represents the views of the company as a whole (and not merely the individual who has written it). If included, the company signature should be typed on the second line below the complimentary closing. Begin the company signature at the same point as the complimentary closing (except when the indented style is used).

Writer's Name and Title

1. Type the writer's name on the fourth line below the company signature, if used, or on the fourth line below the complimentary closing. Except in the indented style (see Letter Style 5), start typing at the same point as the company signature or complimentary closing.

2. In addition to the writer's name, type his title or the name of his department or both. Good visual balance will dictate the best arrangement (see the four variations below). If a title takes two or more lines (as in the fourth example), block all the lines at the left.

James Mahoney, Director	Ernest L. Welhoelter
Data Processing Division	Head, Sales Department
Charles Saunders	Franklin Browning
Assistant Manager	Vice President and
Circulation Department	General Manager

3. Never type *Miss* or *Mr.* in the signature line unless the writer's given name might be that of either a man or a woman; for example, *Mr. Evelyn Shaw, Miss Reed Noyes.* It is assumed that a woman is *Miss* unless *Mrs.* is clearly indicated in some way.

4. An unmarried woman should simply sign her name.

Sincerely yours,
Constance Booth

5. A married woman or a widow may include *Mrs.* in either her handwritten or her typewritten signature. Her typewritten signature may consist of:

a. Her first name plus her husband's surname. This is the style most commonly used in business.

Cordially yours,
Mrs. Nancy Wells

b. Her first name plus her maiden surname plus her husband's surname. This is the style used by many professional women.

Cordially yours,
Mrs. Nancy Ross Wells

6. A divorcee may use one of these styles:

a. Her first name plus her maiden surname plus her ex-husband's surname.

Sincerely yours,
Mrs. Elsie Hoyt Prince

b. Her maiden surname plus her ex-husband's surname.

Cordially yours,
Mrs. Hoyt Prince

c. Either of the forms used by an unmarried woman if she has resumed her maiden name.

7. A secretary who signs mail for her employer may use either of the following styles, depending on the wishes of her employer and the circumstances involved.

Sincerely yours,   Sincerely yours,
Secretary to Mr. Benedict   R. H. Benedict, Manager

8. If the person who signs for another is not actually the secretary, either of the following forms may be used:

Sincerely yours,   Sincerely yours,
For Mrs. Benedict   R. H. Benedict, Manager

Reference Initials

1. The initials of the typist are usually typed at the left margin, on the second line below the dictator's name and title in the lower case. In a square-blocked letter (see Letter Styles 4–6), the reference initials are typed at the right margin, on the same line as the dictator's name.

2. When the letter is written by someone other than the person who signs it, use the writer's and the typist's initials (not the signer's and the typist's).

Sincerely yours,

Herbert Heymann
President

PBR/jb

3. Do not include reference initials in a personal letter.

Enclosure Notation

1. If an item is to be included in the envelope with the letter, indicate that fact by typing the word *Enclosure* at the left margin, on the line below the reference initials. If more than one item is to be enclosed, use the word *Enclosures* and indicate the number of items. The styles illustrated below are commonly used.

Enclosure	Enclosures:
Check Enclosed	1. Check
Enclosures 2	2. Invoice

Note: In military correspondence, the word *Inclosure* and the abbreviations *Inc.* and *Incl.* are used.

Carbon Copy Notation

1. If the writer wishes the addressee to know that one or more other persons will be sent a copy of the letter, type a cc (carbon copy) notation at the left margin, on the line below the enclosure notation (if used) or on the line below the reference initials. If several persons are to receive carbon copies, the names should be listed according to the rank of the persons or, if there is no difference in rank, alphabetically.

cc Miss Johnson	CC: Mr. A. C. Case	cc: Wells, Inc.
	Mr. R. G. Flynn	

2. If the addressee is not intended to know that one or more other persons are being sent a copy of the letter, type a bcc (blind carbon copy) notation on the carbon copies only—never on the original copy. Any of the forms used for a regular cc notation may be used for a bcc notation.

Mailing Notation

If a letter is to be delivered by messenger or by registered, certified, or special delivery mail, type the appropriate notation (for example, SPECIAL DELIVERY) at the left margin, on the line below the cc notation (or whatever notation was typed last).

Postscript

A postscript should be avoided. It should only be used to express an afterthought; this usage, however, is not effective as it suggests that the body of the letter was badly organized. When a postscript is used:

a. Start the postscript on the second line below the cc notation (or whatever notation was typed last). If the paragraphs are indented, indent the first line of the postscript; otherwise, begin it at the left margin.

b. Type PS: or P.S. before the first word of the postscript. (Leave two spaces between the colon or period and the first word.)

c. Use PPS: or P.P.S. (or no abbreviation at all) at the beginning of an additional postscript, and treat the additional postscript as a separate paragraph.

Two-page Letters

1. Use plain paper of the same quality as the letterhead (but never a letterhead) for the second and each succeeding page of a long letter.

2. Use the same left and right margins that you used on the first page.

3. On the seventh line from the top of the page, type a continuation-page heading consisting of the following: the name of the

addressee, the page number, and the date. Either of the following styles is acceptable; however, the second is most acceptable:

Mrs. L. R. Austin   2   September 30, 1970

OR:

Mrs. L. R. Austin
Page 2
September 30, 1970

4. Resume typing the message on the third line below the last line of the continuation-page heading.

a. Always type at least two lines of a paragraph at the top of a continuation page, and leave at least two lines of the paragraph at the bottom of the previous page.

b. Do not divide a paragraph that contains three or fewer lines.

c. Never use a continuation page to type only the closing section of a business letter. (The complimentary closing should always be preceded by at least two lines of the message.)

5. Leave a bottom margin of at least 1 inch at the foot of each page of a letter (except the last page), and keep the bottom margin as uniform as possible on all pages except the last.

6. Avoid dividing the last word on a page.

Spacing and Styles of Letters

1. A business letter is usually arranged in one of the following styles:

a. The *blocked* (modified block) and the *semiblocked* (modified block with indented paragraphs) are the most popular styles (see Letter Styles 1 and 2).

b. The *full-blocked* (extreme block) style is similar to the *simplified* letter recommended by the Administrative Management Society (AMS). (Compare Letter Style 3 with Letter Style 6.)

c. The *square-blocked* style (see Letter Style 4) permits typing more copy on a page.

d. The *indented style* (not illustrated) is outmoded and rarely used.

e. The *hanging-indented* style (see Letter Style 5) is seldom used except in advertising or sales letters.

Punctuation Patterns

1. The body of a business letter is always punctuated with normal punctuation. The other parts of a letter may be punctuated according to one of the following patterns:

a. *Standard* (mixed) pattern (see Letter Styles 1, 2, 4, and 5). A colon is used after the salutation and a comma after the complimentary closing.

b. *Open* pattern (see Letter Styles 3 and 6). No punctuation is used at the end of any line outside the body of the letter unless that line ends with an abbreviation.

c. *Close* (full) pattern. Each line outside the body of the letter ends with a punctuation mark.

Letter Style 1. The blocked style is the standard letter style. Paragraphs begin at the left margin, and punctuation is standard.

Blocked
The most popular
Letter Style   With foreign address and quotation

March 10, 19___

Mr. Philip Watkins
Watkins & Matthews, Ltd.
139 Wellington Street
Ottawa 2, Ontario
CANADA

Dear Mr. Watkins:

It is current practice in American business letters to display quotations and similar data in a special paragraph, like this:

> The paragraph is indented five spaces on both sides and is preceded and followed by one ordinary blank line space.

> If it is necessary to use more paragraphs for the quotation, then a standard single blank line is left between paragraphs.

We show the mail service (on the second line below the date) only if we are sending the correspondence by some special service, such as special delivery or registered, and we do so only to get the fact indicated on our file copy of the correspondence.

Sincerely yours,

Donald L. Fowler
Assistant Director
Bureau of Information
and Public Relations

rtf

Letter Style 2. The semiblocked style is the same as the blocked style except that the first line of each paragraph is indented.

Semiblocked
Conservative, Executive
Letter Style   With attention line and cc notation

March 7, 19—

Savard, Foster & Company
171 Westminster Street
Providence, RI 02904

ATTENTION TRAINING DIRECTOR

Gentlemen:

      For a letter design that is both standard and distinctive, try this style: semiblocked (one of the two most popular styles) with the paragraphs indented *ten* spaces (instead of the usual five).
      This letter also shows you an alternative arrangement for the attention line: centered, in all capitals (instead of being blocked at the left margin and underscored). In two respects, however, the use of the attention line here is standard: it is accompanied, as it should be, by the salutation *Gentlemen,* and it is typed *above* the salutation.
      Worth noting also in this letter are the following: (1) positioning the date at the center as an alternative to ending it at the right margin; (2) the use of standard punctuation, which calls for a colon after the salutation and a comma after the complimentary closing; and (3) the use of the carbon copy notation at the bottom to indicate to whom copies of the letter are being sent.

Cordially yours,

Louise R. Adams, Director

rtf

cc Miss Filene
   Dr. Young

Letter Style 3. The full-blocked style is the fastest style to type. Notice that each line begins at the left margin.

Full-Blocked
Vigorous, Aggressive
Letter Style   With subject line and open punctuation

March 16, 19___

Mr. Roger S. Patterson
Western Life Company
2867 East Fourth Street
Cincinnati, OH 45202

Dear Mr. Patterson

Subject: Form of a Full-Blocked Letter

This letter is set up in the full-blocked style, in which every line begins at the left margin. A few companies modify it by moving the date to the right, but most firms use it as shown here. Because this style is the fastest to type, it is considered very modern. It is natural, although not necessary, to use open punctuation with this style of letter.

This letter also illustrates one arrangement of the subject line, which may be used with any style of letter. Like an attention line, a subject line may be typed with underscores or capitals. In a full-blocked letter, it *must* be blocked; in other letter styles, it may be blocked or centered. It always appears after the salutation and before the body, for it is considered a part of the body.

Legal firms and the legal departments of companies sometimes prefer to use the Latin terms *Re* or *In Re* instead of the English word *Subject*.

Cordially yours

Mary Ellen Smith
Reference Department

rtf
Enclosure

Letter Style 4. The square-blocked style allows more copy to be typed on a page because the date and other notations are typed in the right corner margins.

Square-Blocked
The Efficient Space-Saver
Letter Style   With subject line and "corner fillers"

Mrs. Truda Tracy George   March 7, 19___
President, Pi Omega Pi
California State College
San Diego, CA 92101

Dear Mrs. George:

          SUBJECT: THE SQUARE-BLOCKED LETTER

A square-blocked letter like this one is simply the familiar full-blocked letter with (1) the date moved to the right and typed on the same line with the start of the inside address to square off that corner and (2) the reference symbols shifted right to square off that corner.

This arrangement has many advantages. It is almost as quick to type as the full-blocked style. Because it saves lines of space that are otherwise given to the drop after the date and below the signer's identification, you can get seven or eight additional lines of typing on a page. You can see why this is popular among secretaries whose employers dictate rather long letters. Any letter looks shorter when typed in this style. It permits any kind of display, either centered or blocked.

When using this letter style, make it a rule not to use less than a 50-space line; otherwise, the first line of the inside address might run into the date at the right margin. For an ordinary letter, where you do not need to save space, you must remind yourself to start two or three lines lower, lest your letter look too high on the page.

One limitation of the square-blocked letter style is the way it restricts the enclosure notation. If you use *Enclosure* by itself, you can put it above the initials as shown below. If you want to enumerate the enclosures, however, the display would have to be at the left, and then the perfect balance of the squared corners would be lost.

Sincerely yours,

                                                        Enclosure
Mrs. Elsie Dodds Frost   rtf

Letter Style 5. The hanging-indented style is often used in sales letters. All the lines in a paragraph are indented except the opening line.

Hanging-Indented
For Super-Display Salesmanship   With paragraphs and
Letter Style   signer's name displayed

March 9, 19___

Mr. Harold Toupin
Hopkins Senior High School
1001 Highway 7
Hopkins, MN 55343

Dear Mr. Toupin:

Yes, this is a hanging-indented letter, with a key word "hanging" in the margin at the start of each paragraph and with other lines indented.

Yes, this letter style takes attentive production. You set a tab stop some appropriate number of spaces in from the margin and indent all lines except the first one in each paragraph.

Yes, the hanging-indented style is designed solely for sales promotion —this form is too cumbersome for ordinary correspondence. Since the whole point of the display is to feature those paragraph starters, the letter has to be prepared especially to fit this arrangement.

Yes, indicating the signer's name in the reference position, as below, instead of below the space where he signs the letter, is a procedure that may be used with any form of letter. It is a good device to use when a signer has a signature he likes but which is illegible.

Cordially yours,

LETTER DISPLAY, INC.

Vice President, Sales

LTLeslie / rtf

Letter Style 6. The simplified style does not have a salutation or a complimentary closing. The subject line and writer's identification are typed in capital letters.

Simplified
The Efficiency Expert's   With open punctuation and
Letter Style   full-blocked design

March 6, 19—

Mr. Richard W. Parker, Jr.
Humphrey Lumber Company
520 Southwest Park Avenue
Portland, OR 97208

THE SIMPLIFIED LETTER

You will be interested to know, Mr. Parker, that several years ago the Administrative Management Society (formerly NOMA) designed a new letter form called the *simplified letter*. This is a sample:

1. It uses the full-blocked form and open punctuation.

2. It contains no salutation or closing. (AMS believes such expressions to be meaningless.)

3. It displays a subject line in all capitals, both preceded and followed by two blank lines. Note that the word subject is *omitted*.

4. It identifies the signer by an all-capital line that is preceded by at least four blank lines and followed by one—if further notations are used.

5. It seeks to maintain a brisk but friendly tone, partly by using the addressee's name at least in the first sentence.

Perhaps, Mr. Parker, as some say, this form does not really look like a business letter, but its efficiency suggests that this style is worth a trial, especially where output must be increased.

RALPH E. JONES, TRAINING CONSULTANT
rtf

Letter Stationery

1. When typing a business letter:

a. Use letterhead, plain paper, and envelope stationery that is matched in size, weight, and color. The most commonly used sizes of stationery are given in the following table:

Name	Letterhead Size	Envelope No.	Envelope Size
Standard	$8\frac{1}{2}$ x 11	$6\frac{3}{4}$ or 10	$3\frac{5}{8}$ x $6\frac{1}{2}$ $4\frac{1}{8}$ x $9\frac{1}{2}$
Half sheets	$8\frac{1}{2}$ x $5\frac{1}{2}$	$6\frac{3}{4}$	$3\frac{5}{8}$ x $6\frac{1}{2}$
Baronial	$5\frac{1}{2}$ x $8\frac{1}{2}$	$5\frac{3}{8}$	$4\frac{5}{8}$ x $4\frac{15}{16}$
Monarch	$7\frac{1}{4}$ x $10\frac{1}{2}$	7	$3\frac{7}{8}$ x $7\frac{1}{2}$

b. For carbon copies, use *manifold* (an inexpensive, lightweight paper available with either a glazed or unglazed finish), *onionskin* (a stronger, more expensive paper available with either a smooth or a ripple finish), or *copy letterhead* (lightweight paper with the letterhead and the word COPY printed on it).

c. Use carbon paper of the weight and finish most appropriate for the number of copies you are making, as follows:

Copies	Weight	Finish
1–4	Standard	Hard
5–8	Medium	Hard
9–20	Light	Medium

Note: Many companies provide preassembled "snap-out" carbon packs in addition to loose sheets of carbon and copy paper. The sheets of copy paper are often of different colors in order to facilitate the routing of copies.

Letter Placement

1. On a standard typewriter, 1 inch equals:

a. Ten spaces if the machine has *pica* type.

b. Twelve spaces if the machine has *elite* type.

c. Six vertical line spaces.

Note: If you do not know whether your machine has pica or elite type, type a series of periods and compare them with the ones above. (Proportional-spacing machines provide spacing different from that indicated in a, b, and c above.)

2. The following letter-placement guide is generally used when business letters are typed on stationery measuring 8½ by 11 inches.

a. To determine the margins, estimate the number of words in the body of the letter and then select the appropriate line length and margins as shown in the following table:

LETTER-PLACEMENT GUIDE
(With center at 50 and inside address on fifth line below date)

Length of Letter	Words in Body	Length of Line in:		Margins °
		Inches	Spaces	
Short	Up to 100	4	40 pica	30–75
			50 elite+	25–80
Average	100–200	5	50 pica	25–80
			60 elite+	20–85
Long	200–300	6	60 pica	20–85
			70 elite+	15–90
Two-page	Over 300	6	60 pica	20–85
			70 elite+	15–90

Note: In some offices, one line length is used for all letters, regardless of their length.

° An additional five spaces has been added to the right margin setting in order to avoid frequent use of the margin release key.
+ Rounded off.

b. For the spacing to be used between the parts of a letter, see the paragraphs in which the various letter parts are described.

3. To *lengthen* a very short letter, use any combination of the following spacing techniques.

a. Lower the date (from three to five lines).

b. Allow five to six blank lines between the date and the inside address.

c. Use 1½ lines before and after the salutation, between the paragraphs, between the body and the complimentary closing, and between the complimentary closing and the company name.

d. Allow four to six blank lines for the signature.

e. Place the signer's name and title on separate lines.

f. Lower the reference initials one or two lines.

4. To *condense* a long one-page letter, use any combination of the following spacing techniques:

a. Raise the date.

b. Allow only two or three blank lines between the date and inside address.

c. Omit the company name, if permitted.

d. Allow only two blank lines for the signature.

e. Raise the reference initials one or two lines.

5. To insert paper into the machine so that the center of the sheet will always be at a preselected centering point:

a. Select a centering point, such as 50 or 40, and position the carriage so that the printing-point indicator is at that point on the carriage-position scale.

b. Fold a sheet of paper in half lengthwise, make a crease at the fold, unfold the sheet, and then insert it into the machine.

c. Using the paper release, loosen the paper and slide it right or left until the crease is at the center of the printing-point indicator.

d. Set the paper guide at the left edge of the paper.

e. Note and remember the point at which the paper guide appears on the paper-guide scale. Then, always check to see that the paper guide is set at that point before you insert paper into the machine.

Addressing Envelopes

1. When addressing an envelope:

a. Always use single spacing and blocked style.

b. Always type the city, state, and ZIP Code on one line. Leave one space between the state and the ZIP Code.

c. When using a large (No. 10) envelope, start the address on line 14, about 4 inches from the left edge. When using a small (No. 6¾) envelope or when addressing a postcard, start the address on line 12, about 2 inches from the left edge.

d. If a printed return address does not appear on the envelope, type a return address in the upper left corner, beginning on line 3 about ½ inch from the left edge of the envelope. The return address should contain at least the following information, arranged in three lines: (1) the name of the writer or his company; (2) the street address; and (3) the city, state, and ZIP Code.

e. Type an attention line or a notation such as *Personal* or *Confidential* below the return address. It should begin on line 9 or at least two lines below the return address. Begin each word with a capital letter, and use underscoring.

f. If a special mailing procedure is used, type the appropriate notation (such as *SPECIAL DELIVERY* or *REGISTERED*) in all capitals in the upper right corner of the envelope, beginning on line 9. The notation should end about ½ inch from the right margin.

Folding and Inserting Letters

1. Always check for enclosures before folding letters. Remember that carbon copies may require the same (or occasionally different) enclosures.

2. To fold a letter for insertion into a small business envelope, one can:

a. Fold from the lower edge of the letter, bringing the bottom edge to within ½ inch or so of the top edge before you crease the letter.

b. Fold from the right edge, making the fold a little less than one-third the width of the sheet before you crease it.

c. Fold from the left edge, bringing it to within ½ inch or so of the crease you made in step *b* before you crease the sheet again.

d. Insert the left creased edge into the envelope first. This will leave the crease you make in step *b* near the flap of the envelope.

3. To fold a letter for insertion into a large envelope:

a. Fold from the lower edge, bringing the bottom of the letter up approximately one-third the length of the sheet before you make the crease.

b. Fold from the top edge bringing it to within ½ inch or so of the crease you made in step *a* before you make the second crease.

c. Insert the crease you made in step *b* into the envelope first. This will leave the crease you made in step *a* near the flap of the envelope.

Social-Business Correspondence

1. Social-business correspondence usually differs from that of regular business correspondence in such details as these:

a. The salutation is usually very informal (for example, *Dear Betty* or *Dear Jack*) and is followed by a comma instead of a colon.

b. Numbers are often written according to the "word style."

c. The complimentary closing is usually very informal (for example, *Regards* or *Yours*).

d. The writer's typewritten signature may be omitted, depending upon how well the writer knows the addressee.

e. The reference initials are omitted, and even though an enclosure may be mentioned in the letter, the enclosure notation is usually omitted.

f. Carbon copy and other notations rarely appear in social-business letters.

Forms of Address

1. The following forms of address are correct for government officials; military and naval personnel; Roman Catholic, Protestant, and Jewish dignitaries; and education officials. In the salutations that follow the forms of address, the most formal ones are listed first.

Note: The masculine forms of address have been given throughout. When an office is held by a woman, make the following substitutions:

FOR: Mr.   USE: Mrs. or Miss
       Sir: Madam:
       Dear Sir: Dear Madam:
       My dear Mr. . . . (surname):   My dear Mrs. (or Miss)
                                           . . . (surname):
       My dear Mr. Secretary: My dear Madam
                                          Secretary:
       My dear Mr. Mayor: My dear Madam Mayor:

Government Officials

President of the United States

The President
The White House
Washington, D.C. 20500

Mr. President:
The President:
My dear Mr. President:

Vice President of the United States

The Vice President
The United States Senate
Washington, D.C. 20510

OR:

The Honorable . . . (full name)
Vice President of the United States
Washington, D.C. 20501

Sir:
Mr. Vice President:
My dear Mr. Vice President:

Chief Justice of the United States

The Chief Justice of the
   United States
Washington, D.C. 20543

OR:

The Chief Justice
The Supreme Court
Washington, D.C. 20543

Sir:
My dear Mr. Chief Justice:

Cabinet Member

The Honorable . . . (full name)
Secretary of . . . (department)
Washington, D.C. ZIP Code

OR:

The Secretary of . . . (department)
Washington, D.C. ZIP Code

Sir:
Dear Sir:
My dear Mr. Secretary:

United States Senator

The Honorable . . . (full name)
The United States Senate
Washington, D.C. 20510

Sir:
Dear Sir:
My dear Senator:
Dear Senator:

United States Congressman

The Honorable . . . (full name)
House of Representatives
Washington, D.C. 20515

OR:

The Honorable . . . (full name)
Representative in Congress
City, State

Sir:
Dear Sir:
My dear Mr. . . . :
Dear Mr. . . . :

Governor

In Massachusetts, New Hampshire, and by courtesy in some
other states:

His Excellency the Governor
   of . . .
State Capital, State

   In other states:

The Honorable . . . (full name)
Governor of . . .
State Capital, State

Sir:
Dear Sir:
My dear Governor:
Dear Governor . . . :

State Senator

The Honorable . . . (full name)
The State Senate
State Capital, State

Sir:
Dear Sir:
My dear Senator:
Dear Senator . . . :

State Representative or Assemblyman

The Honorable . . . (full name)
House of Representatives
   (or The State Assembly)
State Capital, State

Sir:
Dear Sir:
My dear Mr. . . . :
Dear Mr. . . . :

Mayor

The Honorable . . . (full name)
Mayor of . . . (city)
City, State

OR:

The Mayor of the City of . . .
City, State

Sir:
Dear Sir:
My dear Mr. Mayor:
Dear Mr. Mayor:
Dear Mayor . . . :

Military and Naval Personnel

The addresses of both officers and enlisted men in the Armed
Forces should include title of rank, full name followed by the
initials USA, USN, etc., and address. Below are some specific examples together with the appropriate salutations.

Army Officers

Lieutenant General . . . (full name), USA
Address

Sir:
Dear Sir:
My dear General . . . :
    (*Not:* My dear Lieutenant General . . . :)
Dear General . . . :

For Officers below the rank of Captain, use:

Dear Sir:
My dear Lieutenant . . . :
Dear Lieutenant . . . :

Naval Officers

Admiral . . . (full name), USN
Address

Sir:
Dear Sir:
My dear Admiral . . . :
Dear Admiral . . . :

For Officers below the rank of Commander, use:

Dear Sir:
My dear Mr. . . . :
Dear Mr. . . . :

Enlisted Men

Sergeant . . . (full name), USA
Address
Seaman . . . (full name), USN
Address

Dear Sir:
My dear Sergeant (or Seaman) . . . :
Dear Sergeant (or Seaman) . . . :

Roman Catholic Dignitaries

Cardinal

His Eminence . . . (given name)
    Cardinal . . . (surname)
Address

Your Eminence:

Archbishop and Bishop

The Most Reverend . . . (full name)
Archbishop (or Bishop) of . . . (place)
Address

Your Excellency:

Monsignor

The Right Reverend Monsignor . . . (full name)
Address

Right Reverend Monsignor:
Dear Monsignor:

Priest

Reverend . . . , (full name,
    followed by initials of order)
Address

Reverend Father:
Dear Father . . . :

Mother Superior

The Reverend Mother Superior
Convent of . . .
Address

OR:

Reverend Mother . . . , (name,
    followed by initials of order)
Address

Reverend Mother:
Dear Reverend Mother:
My dear Reverend Mother . . . :
Dear Reverend Mother . . . :

Sister

Sister . . . , (name, followed by
    initials of order)
Address

My dear Sister:
Dear Sister:
My dear Sister . . . :
Dear Sister . . . :

Protestant Dignitaries

Protestant Episcopal Bishop

The Right Reverend . . . (full name)
Bishop of . . . (place)
Address

Right Reverend and dear Sir:
My dear Bishop . . . :
Dear Bishop . . . :

Protestant Episcopal Dean

The Very Reverend . . . (full name)
Dean of . . .
Address

Very Reverend Sir:
My dear Mr. Dean:
My dear Dean:
Dear Dean . . . :

Methodist Bishop

The Reverend . . . (full name)
Bishop of . . .
Address

Reverend Sir:
Dear Sir:
My dear Bishop . . . :
Dear Bishop . . . :

Clergyman with Doctor's Degree

The Reverend Dr. . . . (full name)
Address

OR:

The Reverend . . . (full name), D.D.
Address

Reverend Sir:
Dear Sir:
My dear Dr. . . . :
Dear Dr. . . . :

Clergyman without Doctor's Degree

The Reverend . . . (full name)
Address

Reverend Sir:
Dear Sir:
My dear Mr. . . . :
Dear Mr. . . . :

Jewish Dignitaries

Rabbi with Doctor's Degree

Rabbi . . . (full name), D.D.
Address

OR:

Dr. . . . (full name)
Address

Reverend Sir:
Dear Sir:
My dear Rabbi (or Dr.) . . . :
Dear Rabbi (or Dr.) . . . :

Rabbi without Doctor's Degree

Rabbi . . . (full name)
Address

OR:

Reverend . . . (full name)
Address

Reverend Sir:
Dear Sir:
My dear Rabbi . . . :
Dear Rabbi . . . :

Education Officials

President of a College or University

. . . , (full name, followed by highest degree)
President . . . (name of college)
Address

OR:

Dr. . . . (full name)
President . . . (name of college)
Address

Dear Sir:
My dear President . . . :
Dear Dr. . . . :

Professor

Professor . . . (full name)
Department of . . .
. . . (name of college)
Address

OR:

. . . , (full name, followed by highest degree)
Department of . . .
. . . (name of college)
Address

Dear Sir:
My dear Professor (or Dr.) . . . :
Dear Professor (or Dr.) . . . :
Dear Mr. . . . :

Superintendent of Schools

Mr. (or Dr.) . . . (full name)
Superintendent of . . . Schools
Address

Dear Sir:
My dear Mr. . . . :
Dear Mr. (or Dr.) . . . :

Member of Board of Education

Mr. . . . (full name)
Member . . . (name of city)
    Board of Education
Address

Dear Sir:
My dear Mr. . . . :
Dear Mr. . . . :

Principal

Mr. (or Dr.) . . . (full name)
Principal . . . (name of school)
Address

Dear Sir:
My dear Mr. . . . :
Dear Mr. (or Dr.) . . . :

Teacher

Mr. (or Dr.) . . . (full name)
. . . (name of school)
Address

Dear Sir:
My dear Mr. . . . :
Dear Mr. (or Dr.) . . . :

The Authors

Rosemary Fruehling was born in Minnesota and received an M.A. from the University of Minnesota. Her teaching experience ranges from various programs at the high school level to graduate school seminars at leading universities. She is well known as a lecturer in the field of business and office education and has served as a consultant to a number of major corporations and state departments of education. In addition to writing articles for professional journals, she co-authored *Business Correspondence/30*, a textbook in business communications.

Mrs. Fruehling is now an Associate Professor in the Secretarial Science Department at The County College of Morris in Dover, New Jersey.

Sharon Bouchard, who holds a B.S. from the University of Minnesota, taught business education at Hopkins Senior High School, Hopkins, Minnesota, for several years, and has worked as a consultant to International Milling Company and General Mills in their in-service training programs. She is co-author of *Business Correspondence/30*. Mrs. Bouchard lives in Minnetonka, Minnesota.